DAY HIKES ON THE
CALIFORNIA
CENTRAL COAST

71 GREAT HIKES

by Robert Stone

Day Hike Books, Inc.
RED LODGE, MONTANA

Published by Day Hike Books, Inc.
P.O. Box 865
Red Lodge, Montana 59068

Distributed by The Globe Pequot Press
246 Goose Lane
P.O. Box 480
Guilford, CT 06437-0480
800-243-0495 (direct order) • 800-820-2329 (fax order)
www.globe-pequot.com

Photographs by Robert Stone
Design by Paula Doherty

The author has made every attempt to provide accurate
information in this book. However, trail routes and features may
change—please use common sense and forethought, and be mindful
of your own capabilities. Let this book guide you, but be aware
that each hiker assumes responsibility for their own safety.
The author and publisher do not assume any responsibility for loss,
damage or injury caused through the use of this book.

Cover photo: Canary Point in Point Lobos State Reserve, Hike 8.
Back cover photo: Soberanes Point, Hike 12.

Table of Contents

THE HIKES

Monterey County

Santa Barbara County

About the Hikes

Day Hikes on the California Central Coast is a guide to 71 great day hikes in the three adjacent counties of Monterey, San Luis Obispo and Santa Barbara. The counties include over 300 miles of Pacific coastline and are home to some of California's most beautiful scenery, including the 80-mile Big Sur coast. The scalloped coastline is dotted with picturesque communities. Trails weave along the undulating coast and around these quaint towns. This guide will take you to the central coast's best day hikes, getting you to the trailhead and onto the trail with clear, concise directions.

The network of hiking trails along the coastal counties lies across some of the most diverse and scenic geography of the state. These 71 day hikes are all found on or adjacent to the coastline. They range from easy to moderately strenuous and have been chosen for their scenery, variety and ability to be hiked within the day. Highlights include oceanfront cliffs and promontories, coves and tidepools, white sand beaches, windswept dunes, streamfed canyons and waterfalls, redwood forests, mountain peaks, wildlife sanctuaries, historical sites and a cliffside lighthouse. The most extensive coastal dunes in California are found along the Pismo Beach coast. State parks include the rugged northern headlands of Point Lobos State Reserve and Montaña de Oro, where you will discover some of the most beautiful coastal scenery anywhere. To help you decide which hikes are most appealing to you, a brief summary of the highlights is included with each hike. You may enjoy these areas for a short time or the whole day.

Heading inland from the coast, the Santa Ynez Mountains rise over 3,000 feet. The Los Padres National Forest stretches along the coast through all three counties, while the Ventana Wilderness lies in Monterey County. The mountains and forests separate the coastal plain from the rolling farmlands, agricultural valleys and mountainous interior of California.

California coastal communities are often as interesting to tour as the undeveloped landscape. Walking paths wind through several towns, connecting communities to nearby beaches and bluffs. Santa Barbara, known as "the jewel of the American Riviera," is a charming oceanfront city surrounded by a diverse landscape and a considerable number of hiking trails. Heading up coast you will encounter several beach communities, including Pismo, Shell and Avila Beaches, located where the expansive dunes meet the rocky cliffs. Continue to Morro Bay, surrounded by wetlands, wildlife and parks. Big Sur, in Monterey County, lies against rugged mountain cliffs along the jagged coastline. At the north end of the county is the Monterey Peninsula, home to Carmel, Pacific Grove and Monterey. These popular destination towns sit along the rocky coastline with tidepools and coves.

Hikes are found within a short drive of any of several coastal communities. An overall map of the three counties and their hikes is found on pages 8—9. Individual county maps are found at the beginning of each county's section, which identify major access roads and the location of hikes in the overall area.

Each of the hikes is also accompanied with its own map and detailed driving and hiking directions. U.S.G.S. maps and other supplementary maps are listed with the hikes and are useful if you wish to extend your hike.

These outstanding day hikes accommodate every level of hiking experience, with an emphasis on spectacular views and breathtaking overlooks. Visitors and locals alike will enjoy the varied ecological habitats and incredible scenery found along the central coastline.

Enjoy the trails and sights!

A note of caution: Ticks may be prolific and poison oak flourishes in canyons and shady moist areas. Bring drinking water, snacks, hats and sunscreen, and be sure to wear comfortable hiking shoes.

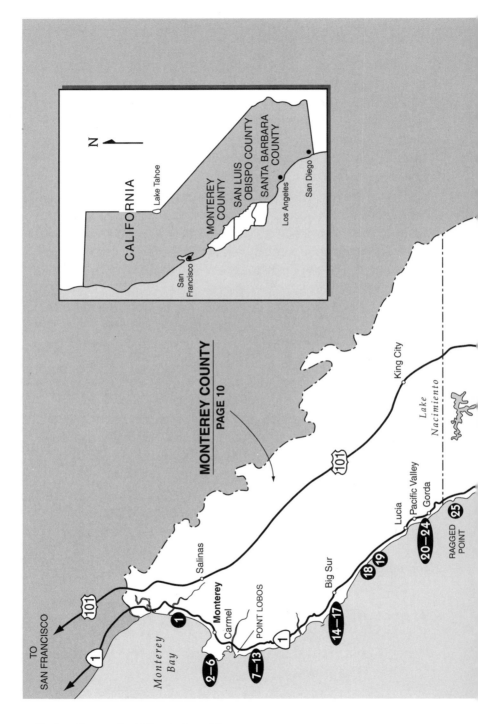

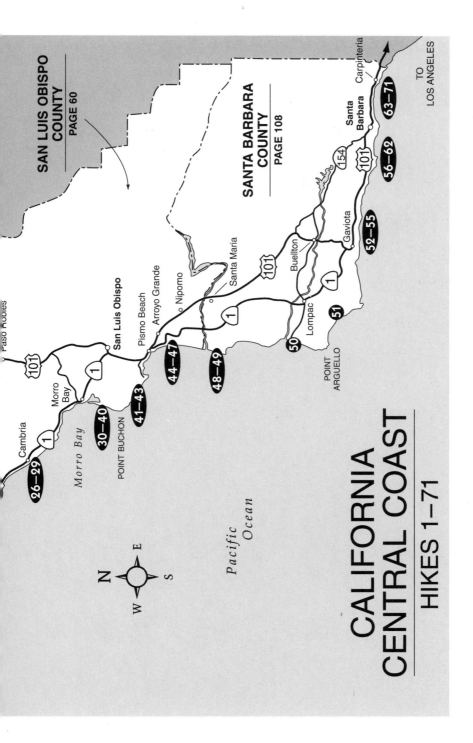

CALIFORNIA CENTRAL COAST
HIKES 1–71

SAN LUIS OBISPO COUNTY
PAGE 60

SANTA BARBARA COUNTY
PAGE 108

TO LOS ANGELES

Carpinteria

Santa Barbara

63–71

56–62

154

101

52–55

Gaviota

Buellton

101

Santa Maria

Nipomo

Arroyo Grande

Pismo Beach

San Luis Obispo

Paso Robles

101

Morro Bay

Cambria

1

26–29

30–40

POINT BUCHON

41–43

44–47

48–49

50

51

Lompac

POINT ARGUELLO

Morro Bay

Pacific Ocean

N
E
S
W

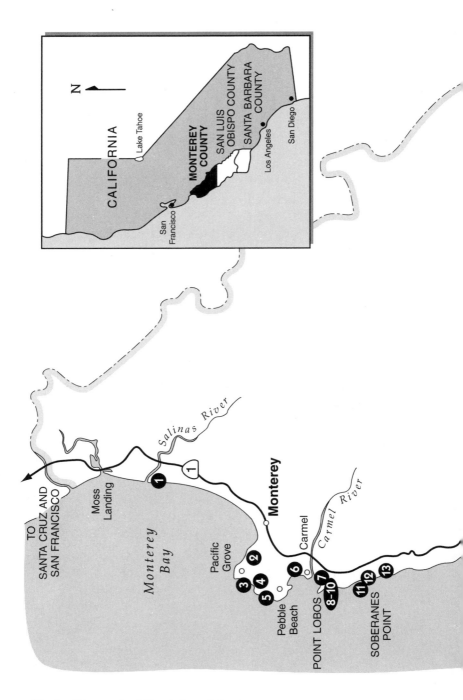

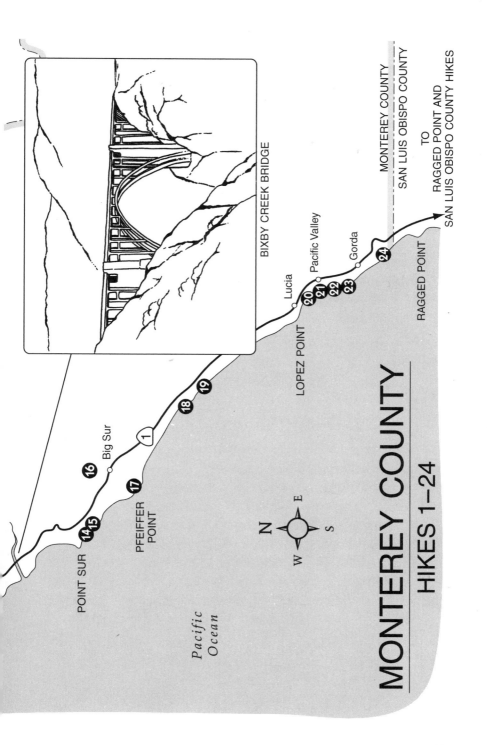

BIXBY CREEK BRIDGE

MONTEREY COUNTY
SAN LUIS OBISPO COUNTY

TO
RAGGED POINT AND
SAN LUIS OBISPO COUNTY HIKES

Lucia

Pacific Valley

Gorda

20 21 22 23

24

RAGGED POINT

LOPEZ POINT

18 19

Big Sur

1

16

17

PFEIFFER POINT

POINT SUR

14 15

Pacific Ocean

N
W — E
S

MONTEREY COUNTY
HIKES 1–24

Hike 1
Salinas River National Wildlife Refuge

Hiking distance: 4 miles round trip
Hiking time: 2 hour
Elevation gain: Level
Maps: U.S.G.S. Marina and Moss Landing

Summary of hike: The 518-acre Salinas River National Wildlife Refuge is a sanctuary for nesting and migrating birds. The hike through the preserve crosses grassland meadows to the bird-filled South Marsh, a brackish lagoon and estuary. A ridge of dunes separates South Marsh from the ocean. The trail continues past undisturbed vegetation-covered dunes to the isolated, sandy oceanfront. From the trailhead, another path leads to the banks of the wide Salinas River.

Driving directions: Drive 13 miles north of Monterey on Highway 1 to the Del Monte Boulevard exit, located between the Reservation Road and Nashua-Molera Road exits. Turn left and drive straight ahead 0.6 miles to the end of the dirt road at the signed trailhead and parking area.

Hiking directions: Walk past the metal gate to a trail junction. The right fork is a short side trip on a two-track path to the banks of the Salinas River. Take the Beach Trail to the left. Head west across the flat grassy meadows to the edge of South Marsh, a lagoon and estuary. Bear left towards the dunes. Cross the north edge of the scrub-covered dunes along the south side of the lagoon, reaching the sandy beach at 0.8 miles. At the oceanfront, follow the sandy shoreline for a little more than a mile to the lagoon at the mouth of the Salinas River, adjacent to Salinas River State Beach. Return along the same route.

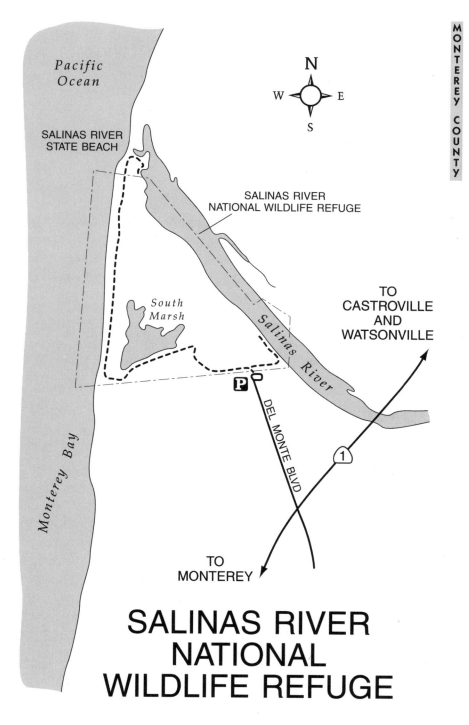

Pacific
Ocean

SALINAS RIVER
STATE BEACH

SALINAS RIVER
NATIONAL WILDLIFE REFUGE

South
Marsh

Salinas River

Monterey Bay

TO
CASTROVILLE
AND
WATSONVILLE

P

DEL MONTE BLVD

1

TO
MONTEREY

SALINAS RIVER
NATIONAL
WILDLIFE REFUGE

Hike 2
Monterey Bay Coastal Trail
Monterey Bay Aquarium to Lucas Point

Hiking distance: 4.6 miles round trip
Hiking time: 2 hours
Elevation gain: Level
Maps: U.S.G.S. Monterey

Summary of hike: The Monterey Bay Coastal Trail follows the beautiful rocky coastline along the blufftop in Pacific Grove. The trail threads through several parks en route to the northern tip of Pacific Grove, passing dramatic rock formations, tidepools, small beach coves and overlooks. The waters surrounding the peninsula are part of the Pacific Grove Marine Gardens Fish Refuge, a national marine sanctuary.

Driving directions: The hike begins by the Monterey Bay Aquarium in Monterey, at the intersection of Ocean View Boulevard and David Avenue. From Highway 1, take the Monterey exit and follow the signs to the aquarium.

Hiking directions: From the aquarium, take the paved path northwest, parallel to Ocean View Boulevard. Follow the coastline past beautiful rock formations and small pocket beaches. Stay to the right of the paved bike path. Continue past Victorian homes and benches along the trail. A side path meanders to the right, rejoining the main trail a short distance ahead. At one mile, Ocean View Boulevard and the trail turn right at Lovers Point. Explore the rocky granite headland jutting out into the ocean. Stairways descend from the grassy picnic area to the sandy beaches of Otter Cove, Lovers Point Beach and Pacific Grove Beach. Turn around here for a two-mile hike.

To continue, follow the cliffside trail past the promontory, weaving through Perkins Park, a landscaped park with stairways to small beach pockets. The trail overlooks the marine refuge past continuous rocky coves and tidepools to Point Pinos at the north tip of Pacific Grove. Return by retracing your steps.

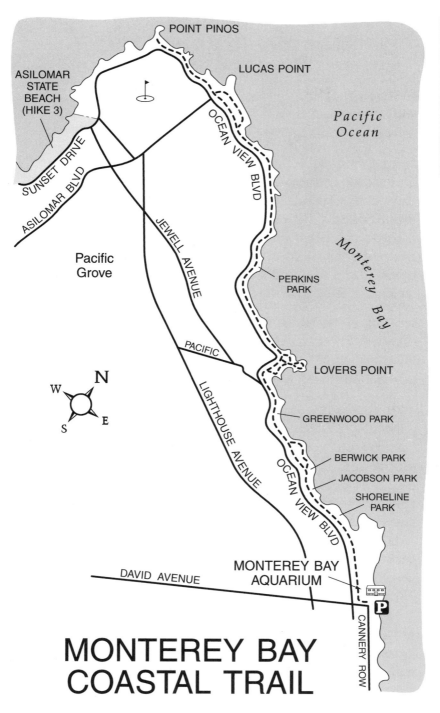

POINT PINOS

LUCAS POINT

ASILOMAR
STATE
BEACH
(HIKE 3)

*Pacific
Ocean*

OCEAN VIEW BLVD

SUNSET DRIVE

ASILOMAR BLVD

Pacific
Grove

JEWELL AVENUE

PACIFIC

LIGHTHOUSE AVENUE

Monterey Bay

PERKINS
PARK

N
W   E
S

LOVERS POINT

GREENWOOD PARK

BERWICK PARK

JACOBSON PARK

SHORELINE
PARK

OCEAN VIEW BLVD

DAVID AVENUE

MONTEREY BAY
AQUARIUM

P

CANNERY ROW

MONTEREY BAY
COASTAL TRAIL

Hike 3
Asilomar State Beach and Coast Trail

Hiking distance: 2.4 miles round trip
Hiking time: 1.5 hours
Elevation gain: Level
Maps: U.S.G.S. Monterey

Summary of hike: Asilomar (meaning "refuge by the sea") State Beach encompasses 107 acres at the windswept, south-west corner of Pacific Grove. The state park has an exposed rocky headland with spectacular views of the Pacific Ocean, tidepools, dunes, cove beaches, a wind-sculpted Monterey pine and cypress forest, sheltered overlooks and boardwalk paths. The park includes the Asilomar Conference Grounds, a national historic landmark.

Driving directions: Asilomar State Park is on the western coastline in Pacific Grove. From Highway 1, take Highway 68 West (which becomes Sunset Drive) to the ocean. Park in the pullouts on the left along the ocean side of Sunset Drive, south of Jewell Avenue.

From downtown Pacific Grove, follow Ocean View Boulevard around the northern tip of Monterey Bay. After rounding the tip, Ocean View Boulevard becomes Sunset Drive. Park in the pullouts south of Jewell Avenue.

Hiking directions: Take the signed trailhead on the gravel paths leading toward the shoreline. To the right is a covered overlook. Follow the meandering trail left (south) above the rocky coves and tidepools, crossing boardwalks and bridges. Numerous connector trails along Sunset Drive join the main path. The trail ends at the south end of the state park by the sandy shoreline adjacent to Asilomar Beach, also known as North Moss Beach, in Spanish Bay. Across Sunset Drive, a boardwalk crosses the dunes and weaves through a forest of Monterey pines to the Asilomar Conference Grounds. Return along the same route.

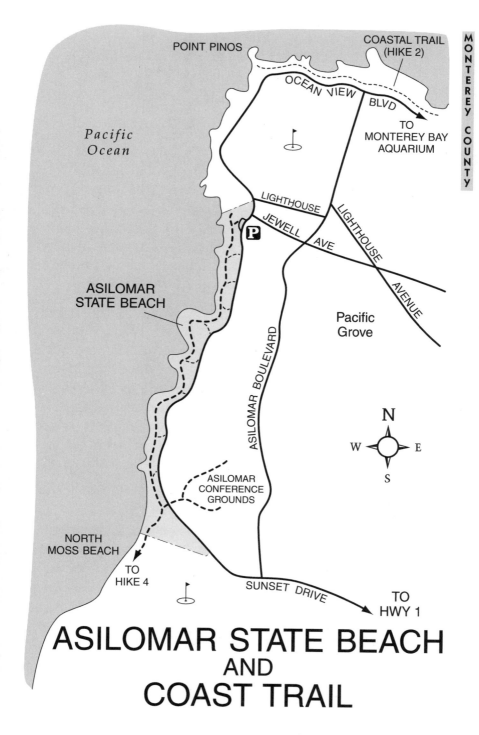

ASILOMAR STATE BEACH
AND
COAST TRAIL

Hike 4
The Links Nature Walk in Spanish Bay

Hiking distance: 1.3 mile loop
Hiking time: 1 hour
Elevation gain: 150 feet
Maps: U.S.G.S. Monterey
Pebble Beach Nature Trails booklet

Summary of hike: The Links Nature Walk begins at The Inn at Spanish Bay. The boardwalk trail crosses the windswept dunes between the Del Monte Forest and the broad, sandy North Moss Beach. The path follows the coastline around the perimeter of The Links at Spanish Bay Golf Course, returning through a forest of Monterey pines and coastal live oaks.

Driving directions: Access to this trail is on the scenic Seventeen Mile Drive, a toll road in Pebble Beach. From the Pacific Grove entrance gate off of Sunset Drive, drive 0.3 miles on Seventeen Mile Drive to the turnoff on the right for The Inn at Spanish Bay. Park in the lot near the entrance to the lodge.

From the Carmel entrance gate off of Ocean Avenue in downtown Carmel, drive 0.2 miles to Seventeen Mile Drive. Turn left and continue 8 miles to the turnoff on the left for The Inn at Spanish Bay. Park in the lot near the entrance to the lodge.

Hiking directions: The trail begins on the ocean side of the lodge. Take the paved path right to the signed boardwalk trail on the left. Head towards the ocean, weaving through the golf course to a boardwalk on the right. Bear right, crossing the dunes to the oceanfront at a T-junction. The left fork is the Bay Nature Walk. Take the right fork on the Links Nature Walk, following the boardwalk north along the coastline. Pass rock outcroppings, tidepools and a beach access on the left at the south border of Asilomar Beach. Continue north for a short distance along Asilomar Beach. Curve inland, crossing over scrub-covered dunes bordered by the golf course on the right and Sunset Drive to the left. Cross a wooden footbridge over a stream, parallel to Sunset Drive. Pick up the signed trail on the right just past the Beachcomber Inn, and head southeast, away from the road. Wind through a Monterey pine forest to Seventeen Mile Road. Parallel the road on the forested path, crossing the entrance road to The Inn at Spanish Bay. Continue to a junction with the Bay Nature Walk. Bear right past a picnic area, completing the loop at the inn.

To extend your hike by one mile, include the Bay Nature Walk in the loop.

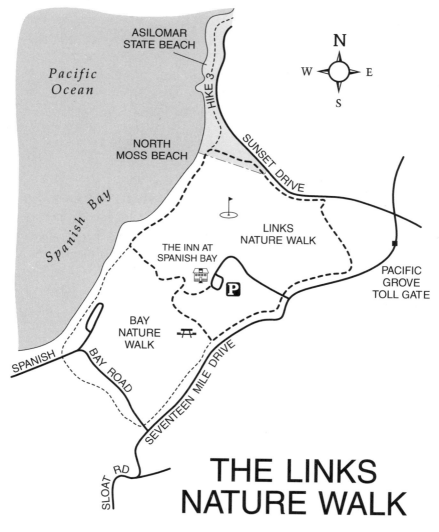

THE LINKS
NATURE WALK

Hike 5
Bird Rock to Indian Village
Pebble Beach

Hiking distance: 1 mile loop
Hiking time: 30 minutes
Elevation gain: 50 feet
Maps: U.S.G.S. Monterey
       Pebble Beach Nature Trails booklet

Summary of hike: The hike to Indian Village begins at Bird Rock, a large offshore rock that is home to numerous shoreline birds, sea lions and harbor seals. The self-guided nature trail follows the coastline towards Seal Rock before crossing the dunes into the Del Monte Forest. The path winds through Monterey pines to Indian Village, a site thought to be used by the Costanoan Indians as a spa before the Spanish missionaries arrived in the 1700s. It is now a large, grassy picnic area with a log cabin.

Driving directions: Access to this trail is on the scenic Seventeen Mile Drive, a toll road in Pebble Beach. From the Pacific Grove entrance gate off of Sunset Drive, drive 3 miles on Seventeen Mile Drive to the signed Bird and Seal Rock Picnic Area on the right.

From the Carmel entrance gate off of Ocean Avenue in downtown Carmel, drive 0.2 miles to Seventeen Mile Drive. Turn left and continue 6.2 miles to the Bird and Seal Rock Picnic Area on the left.

Hiking directions: After marveling at Bird Rock and the coastline, walk south (left) to the signed trail. Continue following the coastline towards Seal Rock. Cross Seventeen Mile Drive and pick up the trail, heading inland. A boardwalk leads through the fragile dunes. Climb the stairs at the east end of the dunes, and enter the shady forest to an unsigned junction. Bear left, following the south banks of Seal Rock Creek. Pass a natural spring on the right, reaching Indian Village, a meadow and picnic area. For the return loop, bear right on the gravel road. Just before reaching the "Gingerbread House" on the right, watch for the trail on the right . Bear right to the junction, completing the loop. Recross the dunes back to the trailhead.

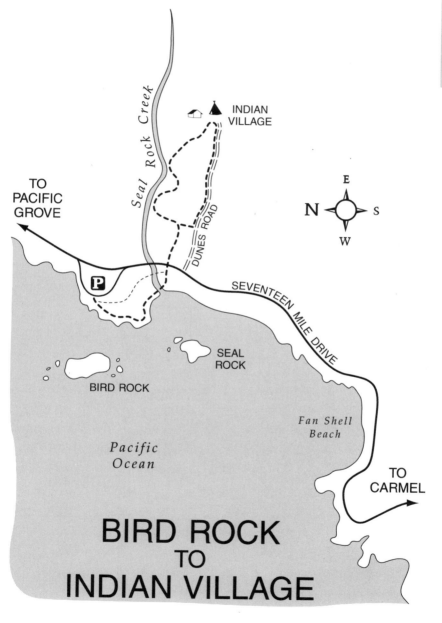

BIRD ROCK
TO
INDIAN VILLAGE

Hike 6
Scenic Bluff Path
Carmel Beach

Hiking distance: 1.4 miles round trip
Hiking time: 45 minutes
Elevation gain: Level
Maps: U.S.G.S. Monterey

Summary of hike: The Scenic Bluff Path is a well-maintained gravel pathway in Carmel. The path parallels Scenic Road on the bluffs above Carmel Beach, with eight stairways accessing the white sand beach. The trail meanders through the shade of Monterey cypress and landscaped gardens to Carmel Point. Throughout the hike are panoramic views of the jagged coastline from Pebble Beach to Point Lobos. This easy stroll is especially enjoyable for watching sunsets over the Pacific Ocean.

Driving directions: From downtown Carmel, take Ocean Avenue west to Scenic Road, located a block east of the oceanfront. Turn left on Scenic Drive, and drive 2 blocks to the parking spaces on the right.

Hiking directions: Take the gravel path south above the sandy beach strand. The path meanders through the shade of Monterey cypress. Every block has a stairway leading down the rocky cliffs to the beach below. At 0.7 miles, the trail jogs a few times, then ends near Ocean View Avenue as the bay curves west towards Carmel Point. To return, take the same path back, or descend on a stairway and follow the sandy beach strand back. Return to the bluffs on any of the stairways.

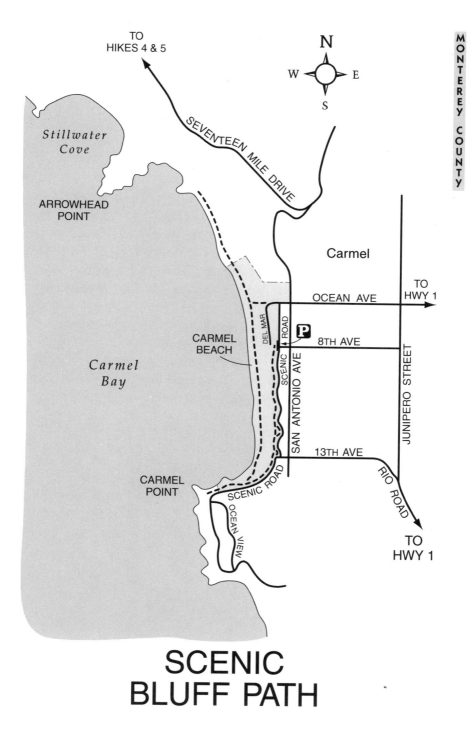

SCENIC
BLUFF PATH

Hike 7
Carmel Meadows to Monastery Beach
Carmel River State Beach

Hiking distance: 2.2 miles round trip
Hiking time: 1.5 hours
Elevation gain: 150 feet
Maps: U.S.G.S. Monterey

Summary of hike: This hike combines beaches and bluff trails along Carmel River State Beach at the south end of Carmel. The Carmel River flows through the north end of this 106-acre state beach, forming a lagoon at a protected bird sanctuary. The beach is bordered on the south by Point Lobos State Reserve. The hike connects Carmel Meadows in the grassland bluffs to San Jose Creek Beach, known locally as Monastery Beach, named for the Carmelite Monastery in the hills above. A short side trip leads to Portola Cross, the site where the Portola-Crespi Expedition erected a cross to signal passing ships in 1769. From the cross are panoramic views of Carmel Bay, the bird sanctuary, the surrounding mountains and Point Lobos.

Driving directions: From Highway 1 and Rio Road in Carmel, drive 0.9 miles south on Highway 1 to Ribera Road. Turn right and continue 0.7 miles to the trailhead at the end of the road.

Hiking directions: Take the hilltop trail past rock outcroppings through grasslands and brush. Follow the blufftop path 0.2 miles to a junction. The right fork descends down steps to a lower path (the return route). Continue along the top above Middle Beach. The path descends to the lower trail and down to the tidepools and rock formations at the beachfront. Follow the beach south, reaching San Jose Creek, which pools into a small lagoon near Monastery Beach. The serrated cliffs of Point Lobos extend west out into the ocean. Return back to the tidepools, and take the lower trail, passing below a few homes to a junction at the base of a hill. The right fork is the return route. First, bear left up the hill for a short detour to Portola-Crespi

Cross and a scenic vista point. Return to the junction at the base of the hill, and head up the paved path to Calle La Cruz. Walk one block to Ribera Road. Go right a quarter mile to the trailhead at the end of the road.

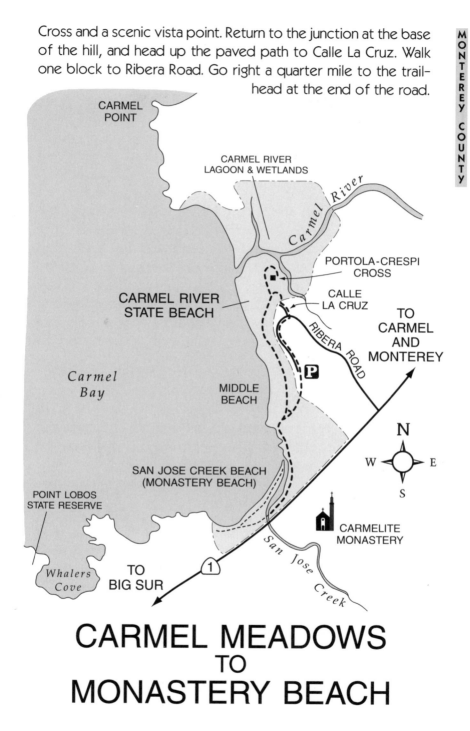

CARMEL MEADOWS
TO
MONASTERY BEACH

Hike 8
North Shore Trail
Point Lobos State Reserve

Hiking distance: 2.8 miles round trip
Hiking time: 1.5 hours
Elevation gain: 250 feet
Maps: U.S.G.S. Monterey
Point Lobos State Reserve map

Summary of hike: The North Shore Trail follows the exposed, rugged northern headlands past sheer granite cliffs and coves in Point Lobos State Reserve. A spur trail leads to an overlook of Guillemot Island, a rocky offshore nesting site for seabirds. A second spur trail leads to Cypress Cove to view Old Veteran, a windswept, gnarled Monterey cypress clinging to the cliffs of the cove. The main trail winds through a canopy of Monterey pines and cypress draped with veils of lichen.

Driving directions: From Highway 1 and Rio Road in Carmel, drive 2.2 miles south on Highway 1 to the signed Point Lobos State Reserve entrance. Turn right (west) to the entrance kiosk. Continue 0.1 mile to the Whalers Cove turnoff. Turn right and drive 0.3 miles to the parking area at the end of the road. An entrance fee is required.

From the ranger station in Big Sur, drive 24 miles north to the state park entrance and turn left.

Hiking directions: Walk up the rock steps at the north end of the parking lot to a junction. The right fork loops around Cannery Point at the west end of Whalers Cove (cover photo). Back at the first junction, ascend a long set of steps, and enter the forest to another junction. The short right fork leads to an overlook of Bluefish Cove. On the North Shore Trail, curve around the cove to a junction with the Whalers Knoll Trail on the left. Continue weaving along the coastal cliffs around Bluefish Cove to a short spur trail leading to the Guillemot Island overlook. Back on the main trail, continue northwest past a native grove of Monterey cypress in East Grove. Cross a saddle past Big Dome to a second junction with the Whalers Knoll Trail. At Cypress Cove, detour on the Old Veteran Trail to view the twisted Monterey cypress and the cove. The North Shore Trail ends in the coastal scrub at the trailhead to the Cypress Grove Trail (Hike 9) by the Sea Lion Point parking area. Return along the same trail.

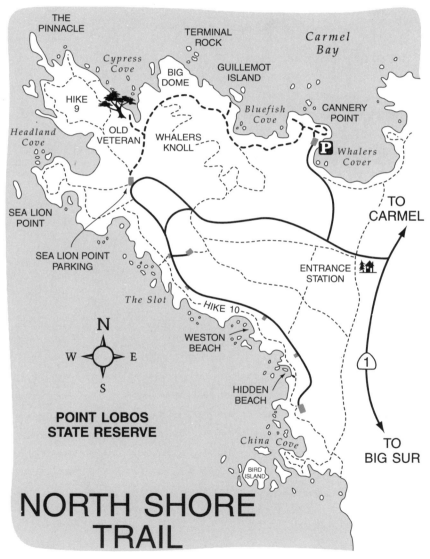

THE PINNACLE

TERMINAL ROCK

Carmel Bay

Cypress Cove

BIG DOME

GUILLEMOT ISLAND

Bluefish Cove

CANNERY POINT

HIKE 9

Headland Cove

OLD VETERAN

WHALERS KNOLL

P *Whalers Cover*

SEA LION POINT

TO CARMEL

SEA LION POINT PARKING

ENTRANCE STATION

The Slot

HIKE 10

1

WESTON BEACH

N
W · E
S

HIDDEN BEACH

TO BIG SUR

POINT LOBOS STATE RESERVE

China Cove

BIRD ISLAND

NORTH SHORE TRAIL

Hike 9
Cypress Grove Trail
Point Lobos State Reserve

Hiking distance: 0.8 miles round trip
Hiking time: 30 minutes
Elevation gain: 100 feet
Maps: U.S.G.S. Monterey
Point Lobos State Reserve map

Summary of hike: The Cypress Grove Trail is a clifftop loop trail around Allan Memorial Grove. The trail passes through one of only two natural stands of Monterey cypress in the world. The hike loops around the cliffs overlooking Cypress Cove, Pinnacle Cove, South Point, Headland Cove and The Pinnacle, a narrow peninsula at the northernmost point in the reserve.

Driving directions: From Highway 1 and Rio Road in Carmel, drive 2.2 miles south on Highway 1 to the signed Point Lobos State Reserve entrance. Turn right (west) to the entrance kiosk. Continue 0.7 miles to the Sea Lion Point parking area on the right side of the road. An entrance fee is required.

From the ranger station in Big Sur, drive 24 miles north to the state park entrance and turn left.

Hiking directions: Two well-marked trails begin on the north end of the parking lot. To the right is the North Shore Trail (Hike 8). Take the Cypress Grove Trail to the left through coastal scrub 0.2 miles to a trail split. Begin the loop around Allan Memorial Grove to the right. Follow the edge of Cypress Cove to a short spur trail on the right, leading to an overlook of Cypress Cove and views of Carmel Bay. Back on the loop, pass through an indigenous Monterey cypress grove. A spur trail at the north end of the loop leads to the North Point Overlook with views of The Pinnacle. Back on the main trail, granite steps lead up to Pinnacle Cove on a rocky promontory with stunning views of South Point and Headland Cove. Continue past South Point and Headland Cove, completing the loop. Return to the trailhead.

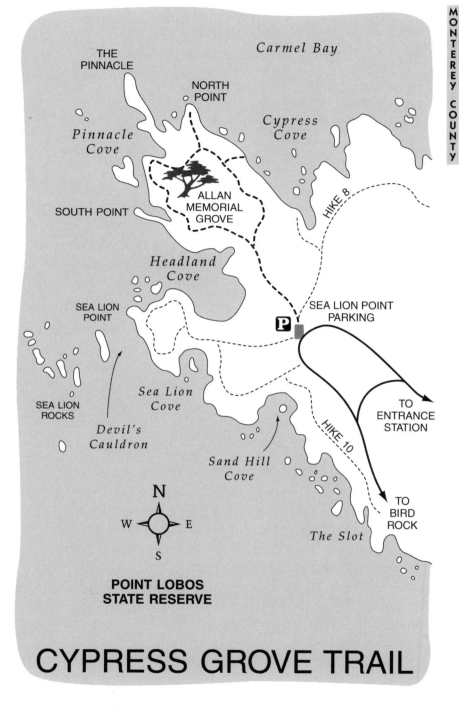

MONTEREY COUNTY

Carmel Bay

THE PINNACLE

NORTH POINT

Cypress Cove

Pinnacle Cove

HIKE 8

SOUTH POINT

ALLAN MEMORIAL GROVE

Headland Cove

SEA LION POINT

P   SEA LION POINT PARKING

SEA LION ROCKS

Sea Lion Cove

TO ENTRANCE STATION

Devil's Cauldron

Sand Hill Cove

HIKE 10

N
W   E
S

The Slot

TO BIRD ROCK

POINT LOBOS STATE RESERVE

CYPRESS GROVE TRAIL

Hike 10
South Shore Trail
Point Lobos State Reserve

Hiking distance: 2 miles round trip
Hiking time: 1 hour
Elevation gain: 30 feet
Maps: U.S.G.S. Monterey
           Point Lobos State Reserve map

Summary of hike: The South Shore Trail explores the eroded sandstone terrain along the jagged southern ridges and troughs of Point Lobos State Reserve. The trail begins near Bird Island and ends by Sea Lion Point, weaving past tidepools and rocky beach coves tucked between the cliffs. The beach coves include Hidden Beach, Weston Beach, The Slot and Sand Hill Cove.

Driving directions: From Highway 1 and Rio Road in Carmel, drive 2.2 miles south on Highway 1 to the signed Point Lobos State Reserve entrance. Turn right (west) to the entrance kiosk. Continue 1.6 miles to the Bird Rock parking area at the end of the road. An entrance fee is required.

From the ranger station in Big Sur, drive 24 miles north to the state park entrance and turn left.

Hiking directions: The signed South Shore Trail begins at the north end of the parking area overlooking China Cove. Head north (right), walking along the edge of the cliffs to a junction with the path to Hidden Beach on the left. Stone steps descend to the oval beach cove. Return to the main trail and follow the contours of the jagged coastline past numerous coves, tidepools and rock islands. A few connector trails on the right lead to parking areas along the park road. At Sand Hill Cove, steps lead up to a T-junction with the Sand Hill Trail. This is our turn-around spot.

To hike further, bear left on a trail around Sea Lion Point and the Devil's Cauldron.

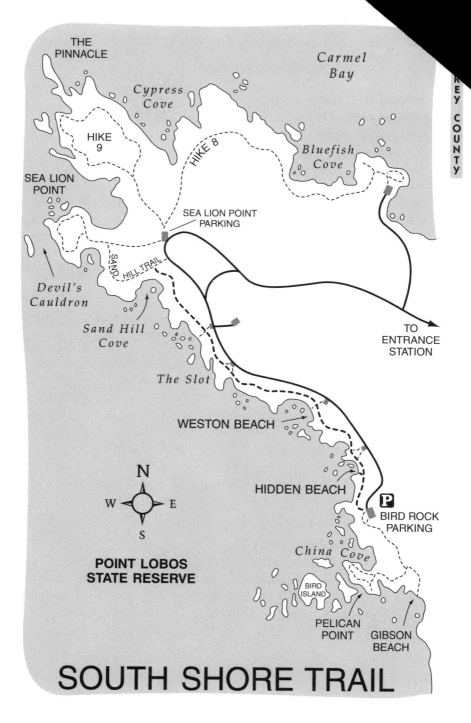

THE
PINNACLE

*Carmel
Bay*

*Cypress
Cove*

HIKE
9

HIKE 8

*Bluefish
Cove*

SEA LION
POINT

SEA LION POINT
PARKING

SAND. HILL TRAIL

*Devil's
Cauldron*

*Sand Hill
Cove*

TO
ENTRANCE
STATION

The Slot

WESTON BEACH

N
W   E
S

HIDDEN BEACH

P
BIRD ROCK
PARKING

**POINT LOBOS
STATE RESERVE**

China Cove

BIRD
ISLAND

PELICAN
POINT

GIBSON
BEACH

REY COUNTY

SOUTH SHORE TRAIL

Hike 11
Soberanes Canyon Trail
Garrapata State Park

Distance: 3 miles round trip
Hiking time: 1.5 hours
Elevation gain: 900 feet
Maps: U.S.G.S. Soberanes Point
        Garrapata State Park map

Summary of hike: The Soberanes Canyon Trail follows Soberanes Creek up the wet, narrow canyon through magnificent stands of huge redwoods. The trail crosses Soberanes Creek seven times before climbing up to the head of the canyon. At the top, the trail emerges onto the dry, chaparral-covered hillside with panoramic views.

Driving directions: From Highway 1 and Rio Road in Carmel, drive 6.8 miles south on Highway 1 to the unsigned parking turnouts on either side of the road. The turnouts are located by a tin roof barn on the inland side of the highway.

From the ranger station in Big Sur, drive 19.4 miles north to the parking turnouts.

Hiking directions: From the inland side of the highway, walk past the trailhead gate, following the old ranch road through a cypress grove. Curve left around the barn and down to Soberanes Creek. Cross the bridge to a signed junction. The left fork leads to Rocky Ridge, the rounded 1,435-foot peak. Take the right fork and head up the canyon along the north side of the creek. Cross another footbridge and curve left, staying in Soberanes Canyon. Recross the creek on a third footbridge and head steadily uphill. Rock hop over the creek, entering a beautiful redwood forest. Follow the watercourse through the redwoods to a lush grotto. The trail crosses the creek three consecutive times, then climbs a long series of steps. Traverse the canyon wall on a cliff ledge, climbing high above the creek. Switchbacks descend back to the creek. Climb up more steps

- THE RIVER INN
  LIVE MUSIC
     ON SUNDAY
- "right" ~~off~~ or
  Highway 1 south
  TOWARDS.

- GOOD FOOD.
  1-800- 548-3610

to the head of the canyon. The lush canyon gives way to the dry sage-covered hills and an unsigned trail split. This is our turnaround spot.

For a longer hike, take the left fork up the steep exposed slopes towards Rocky Ridge, returning on the Rocky Ridge Trail.

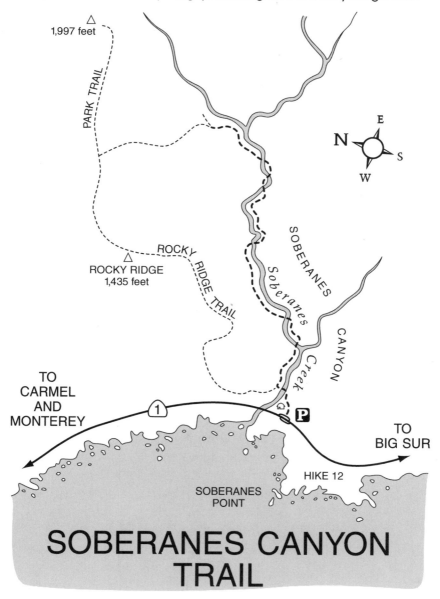

SOBERANES CANYON
TRAIL

Hike 12
Soberanes Point Trails
Garrapata State Park

Hiking distance: 1.8 miles round trip
Hiking time: 1 hour
Elevation gain: 200 feet
Maps: U.S.G.S. Soberanes Point
        Garrapata State Park map

Summary of hike: Undeveloped Garrapata State Park stretches along four miles of scenic coastline and extends into the inland mountains. These coastal bluff trails along Soberanes Point lead to a myriad of crenulated coves, hidden beaches and rocky points (back cover photo). Soberanes Point, a popular whale-watching spot, is a serrated headland backed by Whale Peak, a 280-foot hill overlooking the Pacific. The trail circles the headland, then climbs Whale Peak. From the summit are 360-degree panoramic views from Yankee Point in the north to Point Sur in the south.

Driving directions: From Highway 1 and Rio Road in Carmel, drive 6.8 miles south on Highway 1 to the unsigned parking turnouts on both sides of the road. The turnouts are located by a tin roof barn on the inland side of the highway.

From the ranger station in Big Sur, drive 19.4 miles north to the parking turnouts.

Hiking directions: Walk through the trailhead gate on the ocean side of the highway, bearing left through a grove of cypress trees. Continue south towards Soberanes Point and Whale Peak, curving around the north side of the peak to an unsigned junction. The left fork circles the base of the hill. Take the right fork west along the coastal terrace to the northwest end of Soberanes Point. Follow the ocean cliffs to the southern point. From the south end, the trail returns toward Highway 1 by a gate. Stay on the footpath to the left, following the hillside trail to an unsigned junction. The left fork climbs a quarter-mile up to the grassy ridge of Whale Peak. A trail follows the crest to the two summits. Return to the base of the hill and continue to the north to complete the loop. Go to the right, back to the trailhead.

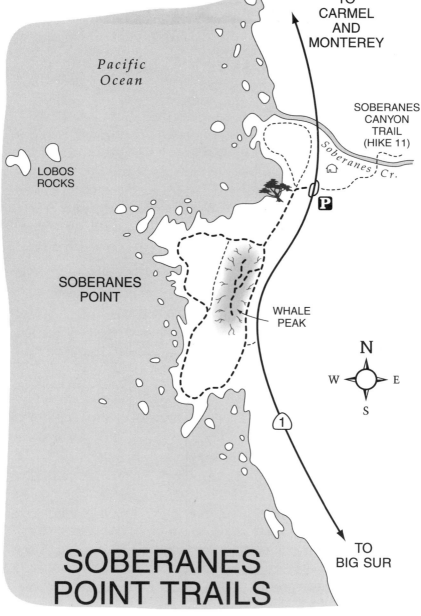

TO
CARMEL
AND
MONTEREY

SOBERANES
CANYON
TRAIL
(HIKE 11)

Soberanes Cr.

*Pacific
Ocean*

LOBOS
ROCKS

P

SOBERANES
POINT

WHALE
PEAK

N

W ↔ E

S

1

TO
BIG SUR

SOBERANES POINT TRAILS

Hike 13
Garrapata Beach and Bluff Trail
Garrapata State Park

Hiking distance: 1–2.5 miles round trip
Hiking time: 1 hour
Elevation gain: 50 feet
Maps: U.S.G.S. Soberanes Point
Garrapata State Park map

Summary of hike: Garrapata Beach sits near the southern border of the 2,879-acre state park. The pristine beach is a half-mile crescent of white sand with rocky tidepools. At the south end, Garrapata Creek empties into the Pacific through a granite gorge. This trail follows the bluffs through an ice plant meadow above the beach. Stairways access the beach. This beautiful sandy strand is an unofficial clothing-optional beach.

Driving directions: From Highway 1 and Rio Road in Carmel, drive 9.6 miles south on Highway 1 to the unsigned parking turnouts on both sides of the highway, located between two historic bridges—1.2 miles south of the Granite Creek Bridge and 0.2 miles north of the Garrapata Creek Bridge.

From the ranger station in Big Sur, drive 16.6 miles north to the parking turnouts.

Hiking directions: Walk through gate 19 and descend a few steps. Follow the path to the edge of the oceanfront cliffs and a trail split. To the left, steps lead down the cliffs to the sandy beach. From the beach, head south (left) a short distance to Garrapata Creek and the jagged rocks at the point. To the right, beachcomb for a half mile along the base of the cliffs to the north point. Back at the blufftop junction, the bluff trail heads north, following the cliff's edge into a ravine. Steps lead down to Doud Creek and a trail split. The left path leads to Garrapata Beach. To the right, the trail crosses the drainage. Steps lead back up the bluffs to a junction. Take the left fork to continue along the bluffs. Choose your own turnaround spot.

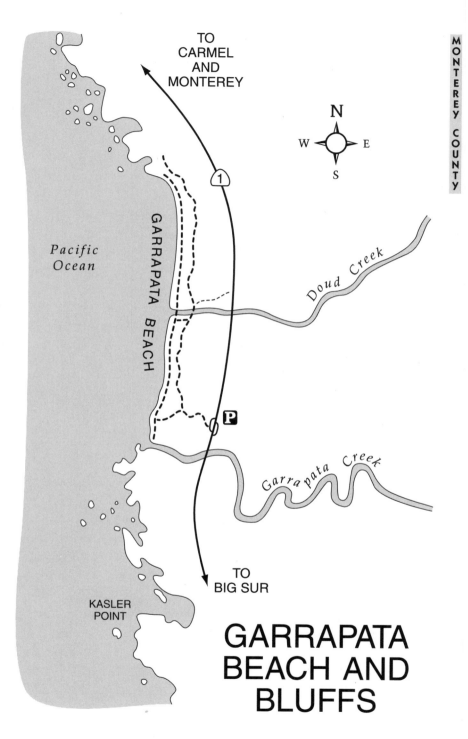

TO
CARMEL
AND
MONTEREY

N
W ☀ E
S

1

*Pacific
Ocean*

GARRAPATA BEACH

Doud Creek

P

Garrapata Creek

TO
BIG SUR

KASLER
POINT

GARRAPATA BEACH AND BLUFFS

Hike 14
Headlands Trail to Molera Point
Andrew Molera State Park

Hiking distance: 2.5 miles round trip
Hiking time: 1.5 hours
Elevation gain: 70 feet
Maps: U.S.G.S. Big Sur
        Andrew Molera State Park map

Summary of hike: The Headlands Trail ascends and circles ocean bluffs and Molera Point in Andrew Molera State Park. From the ridge are views of this diverse park, its numerous hiking trails, Molera Beach, the Point Sur Lighthouse and Cooper Point at the south end of the bay. The trail follows the Big Sur River past Cooper Cabin. Built with redwood logs in 1861, the cabin is the oldest surviving ranch structure in Big Sur.

Driving directions: From Highway 1 and Rio Road in Carmel, drive 21.4 miles south on Highway 1 to the signed Andrew Molera State Park entrance. Turn right and drive down to the entrance kiosk and parking lot. A parking fee is required.

From the ranger station in Big Sur, drive 4.8 miles north to the state park entrance and turn left.

Hiking directions: The signed trail is at the far (northwest) end of the parking lot. Walk past the "Trail Camp" sign and up into a shady grove. Cross a footbridge over a tributary stream, and parallel the Big Sur River. At 0.3 miles, the trail merges with an old ranch road. Bear left, entering Trail Camp, and walk through the campground past large oaks and sycamores. Cooper Cabin is to the south in a eucalyptus grove. After viewing the historic cabin, continue southwest on the ranch road, following the river to a signed junction and map at one mile. The left fork leads to a seasonal bridge crossing the Big Sur River to Molera Beach (Hike 15). Take the right fork on the Headland Trail up wooden steps to the ridge. Walk out to sea on the headlands, circling the point. Return by reversing your route.

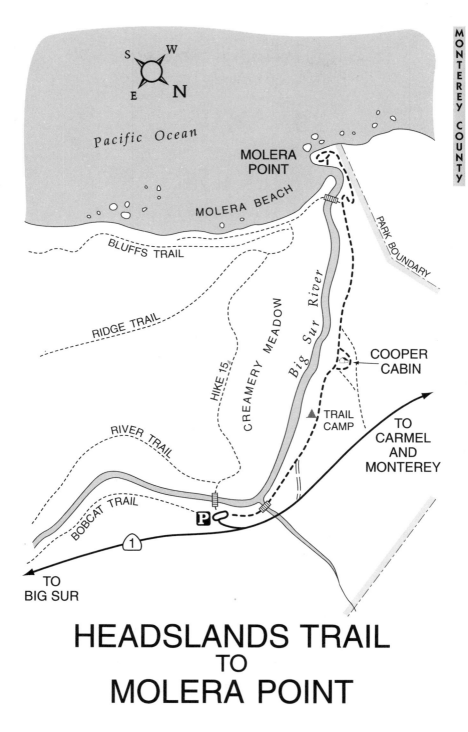

S W
E N

Pacific Ocean

MOLERA
POINT

MOLERA BEACH

PARK BOUNDARY

BLUFFS TRAIL

RIDGE TRAIL

Big Sur River

CREAMERY MEADOW

HIKE 15

COOPER
CABIN

TRAIL
CAMP

TO
CARMEL
AND
MONTEREY

RIVER TRAIL

P

BOBCAT TRAIL

1

TO
BIG SUR

HEADSLANDS TRAIL
TO
MOLERA POINT

Hike 15
Creamery Meadow to Molera Beach
Andrew Molera State Park

Hiking distance: 2 miles round trip
Hiking time: 1 hour
Elevation gain: Level
Maps: U.S.G.S. Big Sur
      Andrew Molera State Park map

Summary of hike: Andrew Molera State Park, the largest state park on the Big Sur coast, encompasses 4,800 acres and extends along both sides of Highway 1. The state park has mountains, meadows, a 2.5-mile strand of beach, and over 15 miles of hiking trails. The Big Sur River flows through the park. Molera Beach, at the Headland Bluffs, is adjacent to a lagoon at the mouth of the Big Sur River. This easy, level hike to the beach meanders through a grassy meadow lined with sycamore trees.

Driving directions: From Highway 1 and Rio Road in Carmel, drive 21.4 miles south on Highway 1 to the signed Andrew Molera State Park entrance. Turn right and drive down to the entrance kiosk and parking lot. A parking fee is required.
    From the ranger station in Big Sur, drive 4.8 miles north to the state park entrance and turn left.

Hiking directions: From the day-use parking area, cross the wooden footbridge over the Big Sur River. Pass the beach trail sign to a trail split. The left fork heads southeast on the River Trail. Take the right fork on the Beach Trail. Cross through Creamery Meadow, a tree-lined grassy meadow, to a T-junction at one mile. The Ridge Trail heads left up the mountain ridge to the south boundary of the park. Take the right fork, staying on the Beach Trail to the back of the sand beach and another junction. The Bluffs Trail heads uphill to the left. Walk to the sandy shoreline. To the north, the beach ends at the mouth of the Big Sur River at the base of Molera Point and the Headland Bluffs (Hike 14). After exploring the beach, return the way you came.

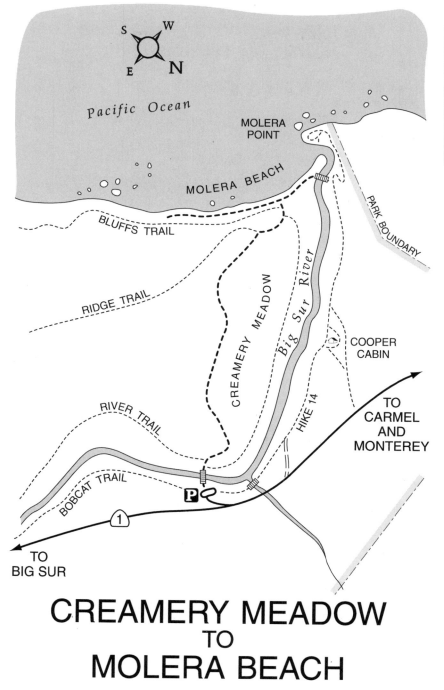

CREAMERY MEADOW
TO
MOLERA BEACH

Hike 16
Pfeiffer Falls—Valley View Loop
Pfeiffer Big Sur State Park

Hiking distance: 2.2 miles round trip
Hiking time: 1 hour
Elevation gain: 450 feet
Maps: U.S.G.S. Big Sur
　　　　Pfeiffer Big Sur State Park map

Summary of hike: Pfeiffer Falls spills 60 feet over granite rock in a small fern grotto. The moist, fern-lined trail follows Pfeiffer-Redwood Creek up the canyon through a redwood forest to the base of the falls. On the return, the Valley View Trail climbs out of the canyon into an oak and chaparral woodland. From an overlook are sweeping views of the Santa Lucia Range, the Big Sur Valley, Point Sur and the blue Pacific Ocean.

Driving directions: From the ranger station in Big Sur, located 27 miles south of Carmel, drive 0.5 miles north on Highway 1 to the signed Pfeiffer Big Sur State Park entrance. Turn right (inland) to the entrance kiosk. Continue to a stop sign. Turn left and a quick right, following the trail signs 0.2 miles to the signed trailhead parking area on the right. An entrance fee is required.

From Highway 1 at Ragged Point, 1.5 miles south of the Monterey County line, drive 48 miles north to the state park entrance, a half mile north of the Big Sur Ranger Station.

Hiking directions: Take the trail at the far (northeast) end of the parking area. Head gradually uphill through the redwood forest. Parallel Pfeiffer-Redwood Creek to the signed Valley View Trail on the left. Begin the loop to the right. Ascend a long series of steps to a signed junction with the Oak Grove Trail on the right. Continue up the canyon towards Pfeiffer Falls as the path zigzags upstream over four wooden footbridges. After the fourth crossing is the second junction with the Valley View Trail on the left, the return route. Stay to the right, climbing two sets of stairs to a platform in front of Pfeiffer Falls. Return to the junction and take the Valley View Trail, crossing a bridge over the creek and another bridge over a tributary stream. Switchbacks lead up the south-facing slope to a signed junction. Bear right towards the Valley View Overlook. Ascend the ridge 0.3 miles to a short loop at the overlook. Return downhill to the junction, and bear right to the canyon floor. Cross the bridge over the creek, completing the loop on the Pfeiffer Falls Trail. Return to the trailhead on the right.

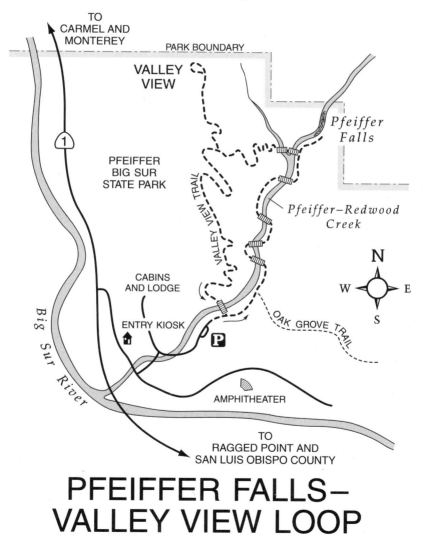

PFEIFFER FALLS–
VALLEY VIEW LOOP

Hike 17
Pfeiffer Beach

Hiking distance: 1 mile round trip
Hiking time: 30 minutes
Elevation gain: Level
Maps: U.S.G.S. Pfeiffer Point
Los Padres National Forest Northern Section Trail Map

Summary of hike: Pfeiffer Beach is a white sand beach surrounded by towering headland cliffs with Pfeiffer Point to the south. Dramatic offshore sea stacks have been sculpted by the wind and pounding surf, creating sea caves, eroding natural arches and blowholes. On the beach, Sycamore Creek forms a small lagoon as it empties into the Pacific. Pfeiffer Beach is part of the Los Padres National Forest.

Driving directions: From the ranger station in Big Sur, 27 miles south of Carmel, drive 0.5 miles south on Highway 1 to the unsigned Sycamore Canyon Road. Turn right and drive 2.2 miles down the narrow, winding road through Sycamore Canyon to the parking lot. A parking fee is required.

From Highway 1 at Ragged Point, 1.5 miles south of the Monterey County line, drive 47 miles north to the unsigned Sycamore Canyon Road, a half mile north of the post office.

Hiking directions: From the west end of the parking area, take the signed trail through a canopy of cypress trees to the wide sandy beach. The beach is divided by Sycamore Creek, which forms a small lagoon. Straight ahead are giant rock formations with natural arches and sea caves. A short distance to the south are the steep cliffs of Pfeiffer Point. Beachcomb along the shore from the point to the cliffs at the far north end of the beach.

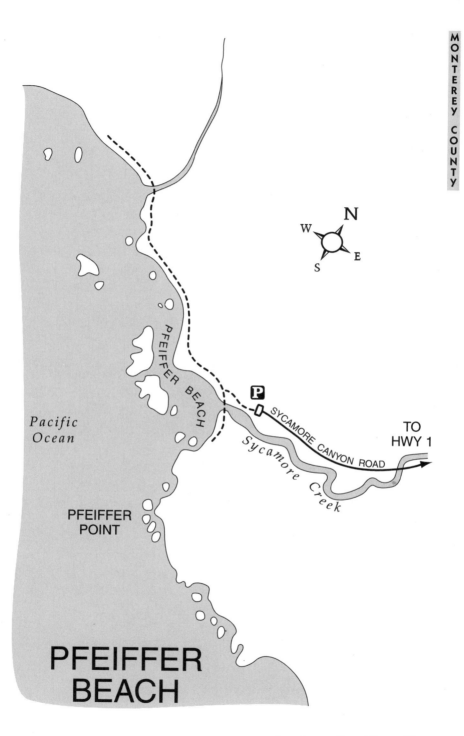

N
W E
S

Pacific
Ocean

PFEIFFER BEACH

P

SYCAMORE CANYON ROAD

Sycamore Creek

TO
HWY 1

PFEIFFER
POINT

PFEIFFER
BEACH

Hike 18
Partington Cove
Julia Pfeiffer Burns State Park

Hiking distance: 1 mile round trip
Hiking time: 1 hour
Elevation gain: 280 feet
Maps: U.S.G.S. Partington Ridge
Julia Pfeiffer Burns State Park map

Summary of hike: Partington Cove sits at the northern boundary of Julia Pfeiffer Burns State Park. The trail to the cove descends down Partington Canyon on an old dirt road. Partington Creek, which carved the canyon, empties into the ocean at the small rocky west cove. A 120–foot tunnel has been cut through the cliffs, leading to the east cove and Partington Landing. The landing was used as a shipping dock for timber in the 1880s by homesteader John Partington.

Driving directions: From the ranger station in Big Sur, 27 miles south of Carmel, drive 8.5 miles south on Highway 1 to the wide parking pullouts on both sides of the highway by Partington Bridge, where the road curves across Partington Creek and the canyon.

From Highway 1 at Ragged Point, 1.5 miles south of the Monterey County line, drive 39 miles north to the parking pullouts. The pullouts are 1.9 miles north of the signed Julia Pfeiffer Burns State Park entrance.

Hiking directions: Head west on the ocean side of Highway 1 past the trailhead gate. Descend on the decomposed granite road along the north canyon wall, high above Partington Creek. The old road weaves downhill to the creek and a junction with an interpretive sign. The left fork follows Partington Creek upstream under a dense forest canopy. Take the right fork 50 yards to a second junction. The left route crosses a wooden footbridge over Partington Creek and leads to the tunnel carved through the granite wall. The tunnel ends on the east cove, where remnants of Partington Landing remain. Return to the junction by the bridge, and take the path that is now on your left. Follow the north bank of Partington Creek to an enclosed beach cove surrounded by the steep cliffs of Partington Point. Return along the same trail.

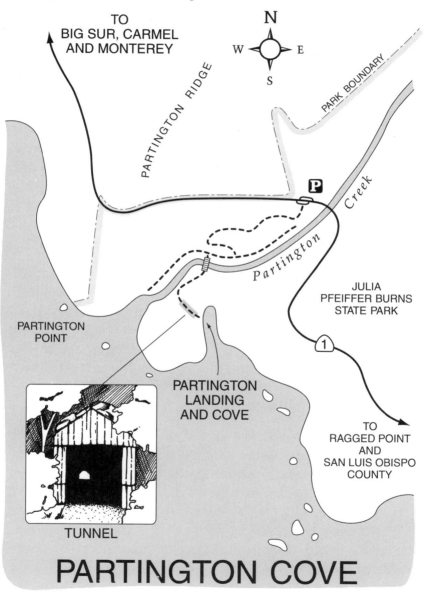

TO
BIG SUR, CARMEL
AND MONTEREY

N

W   E

S

PARTINGTON RIDGE

PARK BOUNDARY

P

Partington Creek

JULIA
PFEIFFER BURNS
STATE PARK

1

PARTINGTON
POINT

PARTINGTON
LANDING
AND COVE

TO
RAGGED POINT
AND
SAN LUIS OBISPO
COUNTY

TUNNEL

PARTINGTON COVE

Hike 19
McWay Falls and Saddle Rock
Julia Pfeiffer Burns State Park

Hiking distance: 0.7 miles round trip
Hiking time: 30 minutes
Elevation gain: 50 feet
Maps: U.S.G.S. Partington Ridge
Julia Pfeiffer Burns State Park map

Summary of hike: McWay Falls pours 80 feet onto the sand along the edge of the Pacific at the mouth of McWay Canyon. The waterfall drops off the granite bluff in a scenic, wooded beach cove lined with offshore rocks. The Waterfall Overlook Trail, a handicap accessible trail, leads to a viewing area of McWay Cove and the cataract on the 100-foot high bluffs. The beach itself is not accessible. On the south side of the bay is a scenic overlook at a cypress-shaded picnic area and environmental camp adjacent to Saddle Rock.

Driving directions: From the ranger station in Big Sur, 27 miles south of Carmel, drive 10.4 miles south on Highway 1 to the signed Julia Pfeiffer Burns State Park. Turn left (inland) and park in the day-use parking lot.

From Highway 1 at Ragged Point, 1.5 miles south of the Monterey County line, drive 37.1 miles north to the state park entrance.

Hiking directions: Descend the steps across the road from the restrooms. At the base of the steps, bear right and head southwest on the signed Waterfall Trail. Follow the north canyon wall above the creek, and walk through the tunnel under Highway 1 to a T-junction. The left fork leads to the Saddle Rock Overlook. For now, take the right fork along the cliffs. Cross a wooden footbridge with great views of McWay Falls pouring onto the sand. Beyond the bridge is an observation deck with expansive coastal views. After enjoying the sights, return to the junction, and take the footpath towards the south end of the bay. Walk through a canopy of old-growth eucalyptus trees high above the falls. Descend to the trail's end at a 206-foot overlook in a cypress grove by the camping and picnic area.

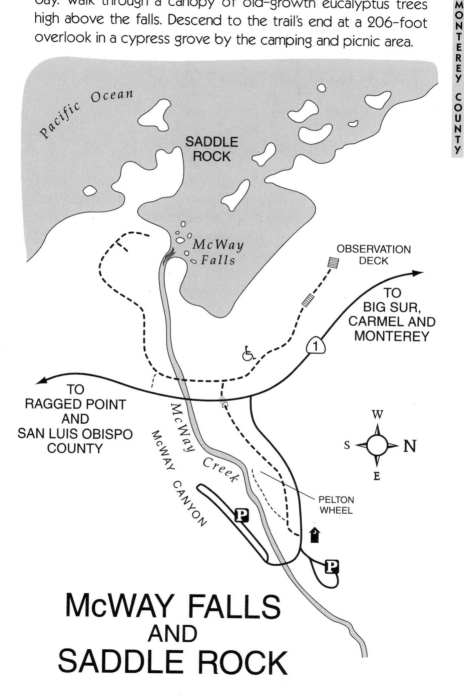

Pacific Ocean

SADDLE ROCK

McWay Falls

OBSERVATION DECK

TO BIG SUR, CARMEL AND MONTEREY

1

TO RAGGED POINT AND SAN LUIS OBISPO COUNTY

McWay Creek

McWAY CANYON

W

S ⊕ N

E

PELTON WHEEL

P

P

McWAY FALLS
AND
SADDLE ROCK

Hike 20
Redwood Trail to Limekilns
Limekiln Creek State Park

Hiking distance: 1 mile round trip
Hiking time: 30 minutes
Elevation gain: 200 feet
Maps: U.S.G.S. Lopez Point
Limekiln State Park map

Summary of hike: The Limekiln Trail leads to four massive stone and steel kilns used to purify quarried limestone into powdered lime in the 1880s. The lime was used as an ingredient in cement. The Limekiln Trail follows the old wagon route used to haul barrels of lime slacked from the furnaces. The hike follows Limekiln Creek and the West Fork up the canyon through redwoods, sycamores, oaks and maples to the giant limekilns.

Driving directions: From the ranger station in Big Sur, 27 miles south of Carmel, drive 25.3 miles south on Highway 1 to the signed Limekiln Creek State Park. Turn left (inland) to the entrance kiosk. Park 30 yards ahead in the day-use parking area on the right. An entrance fee is required.

From Highway 1 at Ragged Point, located 1.5 miles south of the southern Monterey County line, drive 22.2 miles north to the state park on the right.

Hiking directions: Walk up the campground road to the road's north end near the confluence of Limekiln Creek and Hare Creek. Cross the footbridge over Hare Creek in the dense redwood forest to a trail fork. The right fork parallels Hare Creek. Take the left fork, following the contours of Limekiln Creek through the shady forest. Cross a second footbridge where Limekiln Creek and the West Fork flow together. Follow the west bank of the West Fork to a third bridge by cascades and a small waterfall. Continue gradually uphill along the east side of the creek to the four enormous metal cylinders on the right. On the left are waterfalls and pools. Return by retracing your steps.

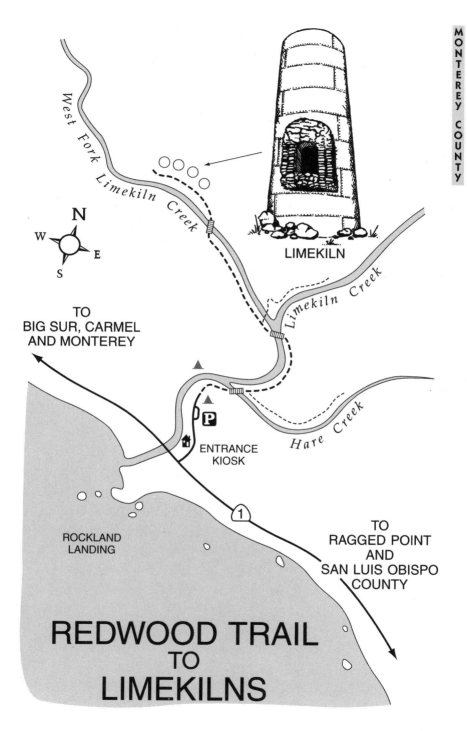

West Fork Limekiln Creek

Limekiln Creek

LIMEKILN

N
W   E
S

TO
BIG SUR, CARMEL
AND MONTEREY

Hare Creek

P

ENTRANCE
KIOSK

1

ROCKLAND
LANDING

TO
RAGGED POINT
AND
SAN LUIS OBISPO
COUNTY

REDWOOD TRAIL
TO
LIMEKILNS

Hike 21
Kirk Creek Beach Trail

Hiking distance: 0.5 miles round trip
Hiking time: 30 minutes
Elevation gain: 150 feet
Maps: U.S.G.S. Cape San Martin
　　　　Los Padres National Forest Northern Section Trail Map

Summary of hike: Kirk Creek Campground sits on the bluffs overlooking the ocean with magnificent views north to Lopez Point. The trail to the beach crosses the grassy marine terrace to dramatic eroded cliffs and rock formations. The path descends the cliffs to a small sandy beach cove with scattered boulders.

Driving directions: From the ranger station in Big Sur, 27 miles south of Carmel, drive 27.2 miles south on Highway 1 to the Kirk Creek Campground on the right (ocean) side. Park in the campground day-use lot (entrance fee required) or in the pull-outs along the highway (free).

From Highway 1 at Ragged Point, 1.5 miles south of the Monterey County line, drive 20.3 miles north to Kirk Creek Campground on the left.

Hiking directions: Follow the campground road, bearing right to the north end of the camp. The signed trail is by camp-site 23. Follow the signed grassy path past the picnic area and through the grove of eucalyptus trees on the bluffs. Descend along the edge of the cliffs. Switchbacks lead down to the small, sandy beach cove. The last 50 feet are a scramble due to erosion. After exploring the cove, return on the same path.

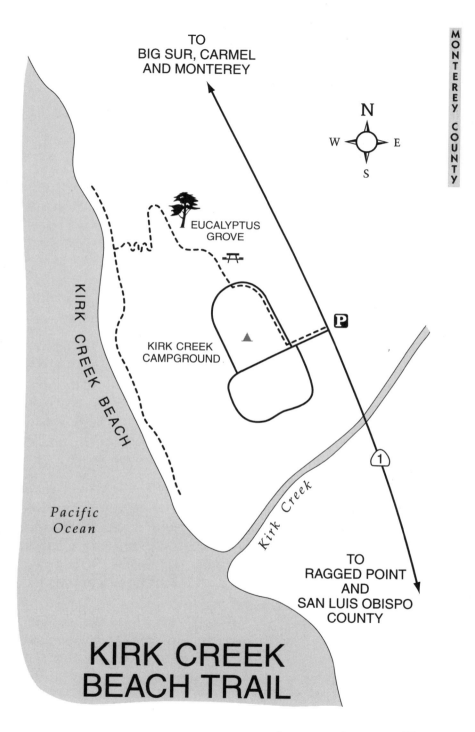

TO
BIG SUR, CARMEL
AND MONTEREY

N
W   E
S

EUCALYPTUS
GROVE

P

KIRK CREEK BEACH

KIRK CREEK
CAMPGROUND

1

Kirk Creek

*Pacific
Ocean*

TO
RAGGED POINT
AND
SAN LUIS OBISPO
COUNTY

KIRK CREEK
BEACH TRAIL

Hike 22
Pacific Valley Flats

Hiking distance: 2 miles round trip
Hiking time: 1 hour
Elevation gain: 50 feet
Maps: U.S.G.S. Cape San Martin
      Los Padres National Forest Northern Section Trail Map

Summary of hike: Pacific Valley is a four-mile long, flat marine terrace. The wide expanse extends west from the steep slopes of the Santa Lucia Mountains to the serrated bluffs above the Pacific Ocean. This hike crosses the grassy coastal terrace to the eroded coastline a hundred feet above the ocean. There are dramatic views of Plaskett Rock, offshore rock formations with natural arches, and the scalloped coastal cliffs. There are numerous access points to the grassland terrace.

Driving directions: From the ranger station in Big Sur, 27 miles south of Carmel, drive 31.5 miles south on Highway 1 to the Pacific Valley Ranger Station on the left. The trailhead is across the highway from the ranger station. Park in the pullouts on either side of the road or in the parking lot at the station.

From Highway 1 at Ragged Point, 1.5 miles south of the Monterey County line, drive 16 miles north to the Pacific Valley Ranger Station.

Hiking directions: The hike begins directly across the road from the Pacific Valley Ranger Station. Step up and over the trail access ladder. Head west across the grassy expanse and past rock outcroppings to the left. Near the point is a rolling sand dune on the right with numerous trails and great overlooks. The main trail stays to the north of the dune, leading to the edge of the cliffs along the jagged coastline high above the pounding surf. At one mile, the trail ends at a fenceline above Prewitt Creek. The trails around the dunes connect with the bluff trail south to Sand Dollar Beach (Hike 23), then circle back to the first junction at the cliff's edge. Return along the same trail.

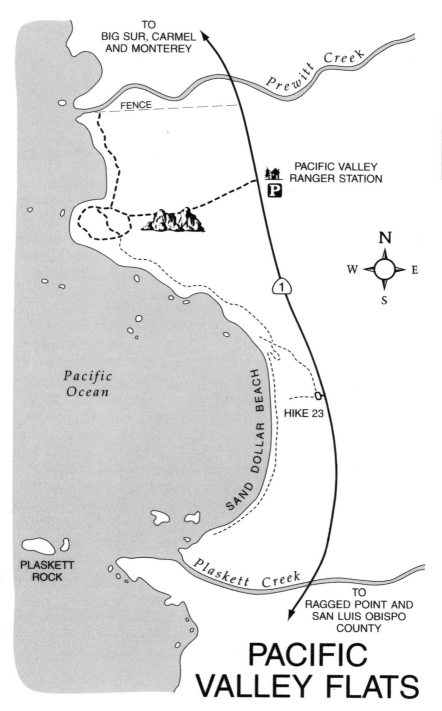

TO
BIG SUR, CARMEL
AND MONTEREY

Prewitt Creek

FENCE

PACIFIC VALLEY
RANGER STATION

P

N
W E
S

1

Pacific
Ocean

SAND DOLLAR BEACH

HIKE 23

PLASKETT
ROCK

Plaskett Creek

TO
RAGGED POINT AND
SAN LUIS OBISPO
COUNTY

PACIFIC
VALLEY FLATS

Hike 23
Sand Dollar Beach

Hiking distance: 0.7 miles round trip
Hiking time: 1 hour
Elevation gain: 150 feet
Maps: U.S.G.S. Cape San Martin
Los Padres National Forest Northern Section Trail Map

Summary of hike: Sand Dollar Beach is a protected horseshoe-shaped sand and rock beach between two rocky headlands. The trail passes a picnic area lined with cypress trees to the steep eroded cliffs and an interpretive cliffside overlook. Plaskett Rock sits off the southern point. There are great coastal views of large offshore rock outcroppings. Cone Peak, at 5,155 feet, can be seen inland in the Santa Lucia Range.

Driving directions: From the ranger station in Big Sur, 27 miles south of Carmel, drive 32.4 miles south on Highway 1 to the parking lot on the right (ocean) side. Park in the lot (entrance fee) or park in the pullouts along the highway (free).

From Highway 1 at Ragged Point, 1.5 miles south of the Monterey County line, drive 15.1 miles north to the parking lot on the left, just north of Plaskett Creek Campground.

Hiking directions: The signed trailhead is at the north end of the parking lot. Walk up and over the stepladder, then descend through a shady picnic area. Cross the grasslands to a junction by a wooden fence. The right fork leads 30 yards to an overlook with an interpretive wildlife sign. Return to the junction and take the left fork down the switchbacks and a staircase to the shoreline. After exploring the crescent-shaped cove, return to the parking lot.

A second trail leaves from the center of the lot. Climb up and over the ladder, and cross the grassy coastal terrace to a cliffside overlook. The meandering path follows the grassy bluffs a half mile south to Jade Cove and one mile north to Pacific Valley (Hike 22).

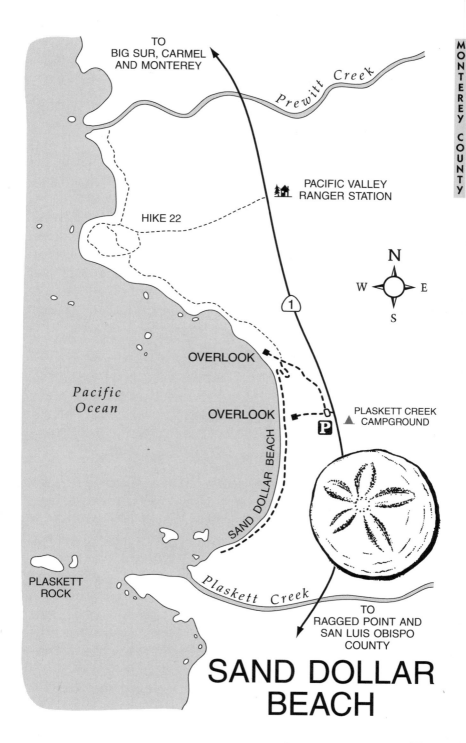

TO
BIG SUR, CARMEL
AND MONTEREY

Prewitt Creek

PACIFIC VALLEY
RANGER STATION

HIKE 22

N
W   E
S

*Pacific
Ocean*

OVERLOOK

OVERLOOK

PLASKETT CREEK
CAMPGROUND

P

SAND DOLLAR BEACH

PLASKETT
ROCK

Plaskett Creek

TO
RAGGED POINT AND
SAN LUIS OBISPO
COUNTY

SAND DOLLAR
BEACH

Hike 24
Salmon Creek Trail to Salmon Creek Falls

Hiking distance: 0.6 miles round trip
Hiking time: 20 minutes
Elevation gain: 150 feet
Maps: U.S.G.S. Burro Mountain

Summary of hike: Salmon Creek Trail is at the southern end of Big Sur country in Monterey County, 2.2 miles north of the county line. The trail follows the first portion of the Salmon Creek Trail to a dynamic waterfall. A short hike leads to the base of Salmon Creek Falls, where a tremendous amount of rushing water plunges from three chutes. The water drops more than 100 feet off the Santa Lucia Mountains onto the rocks and pools. Under the shady landscape of alders and laurels, a cool mist sprays over the mossy green streamside vegetation.

Driving directions: From the ranger station in Big Sur, 27 miles south of Carmel, drive 43.8 miles south on Highway 1 to the signed Salmon Creek trailhead and wide pullout on the left.
From Highway 1 at Ragged Point, 1.5 miles south of the Monterey County line, drive 3.7 miles north to the trailhead on the right.

Hiking directions: Walk alongside the guardrail to the signed trailhead on the south side of Salmon Creek. Salmon Creek Falls can be seen from the guardrail. Take the Salmon Creek Trail up the gorge into the lush, verdant forest. Pass an old wooden gate and cross a small tributary stream. Two hundred yards ahead is a signed junction. The right fork continues on the Salmon Creek Trail, leading up to Spruce Camp and Estrella Camp, primitive streamside campsites two and three miles ahead. Take the left fork towards the falls. Cross another small stream, then descend around huge boulders towards Salmon Creek at the base of the falls. The thunderous sound of the waterfall will lead you to the base. Climb around the wet boulders to various caves and overlooks.

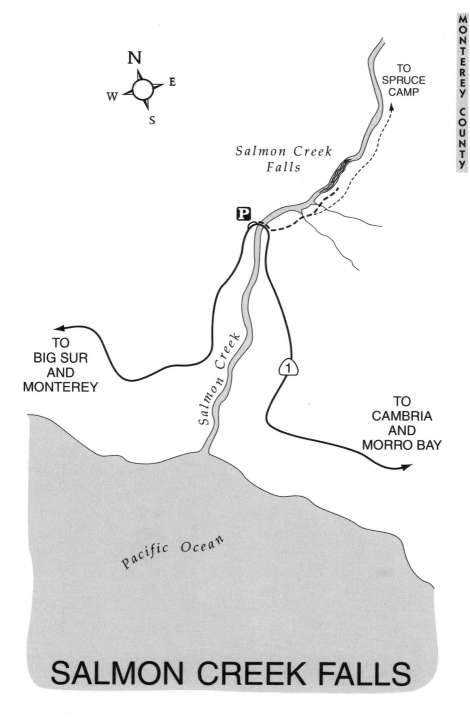

SALMON CREEK FALLS

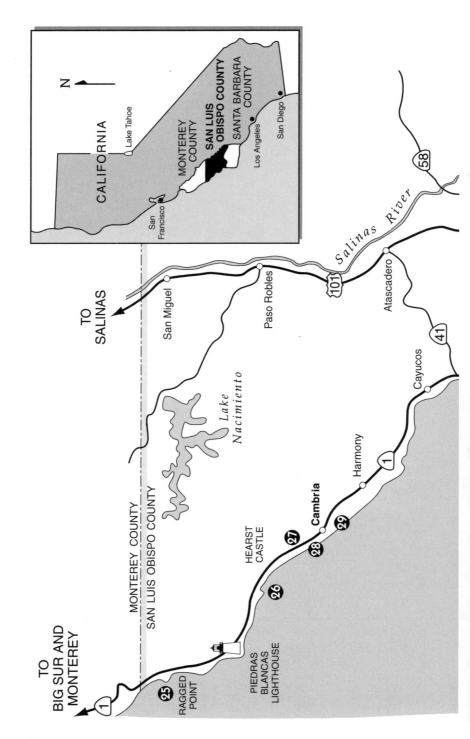

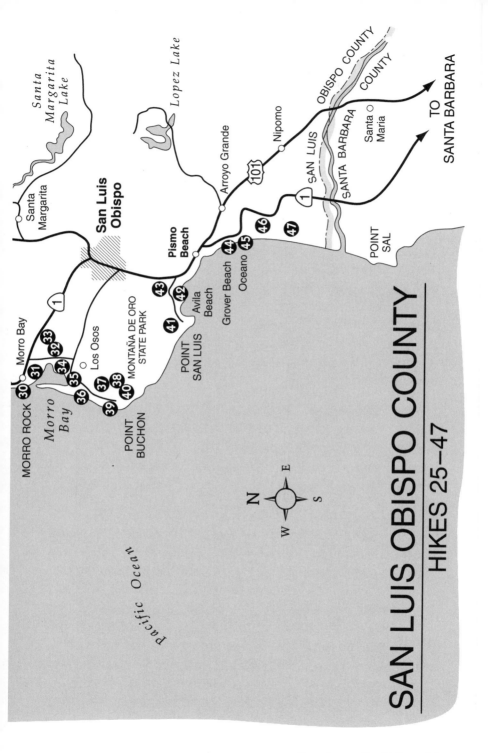

SAN LUIS OBISPO COUNTY
HIKES 25–47

Hike 25
Ragged Point
Cliffside Trail and Nature Trail

Hiking distance: 1 mile round trip
Hiking time: 30 minutes
Elevation gain: 300 feet
Maps: U.S.G.S. Burro Mountain

Summary of hike: The Ragged Point Cliffside Trail cuts across the edge of the steep, rugged, north-facing cliff where the San Luis Obispo coast turns into the Big Sur coast. The Cliffside Trail ends at the black sand beach and rocky shore at the base of Black Swift Falls, a 300-foot tiered waterfall. Benches are perched on the cliff for great views of the sheer coastal mountains plunging into the sea. The Ragged Point Nature Trail follows the perimeter of the peninsula along the high blufftop terrace. There are scenic vista points and an overlook platform.

Driving directions: From Cambria, drive 23 miles north on Highway 1 to the Ragged Point Inn and Restaurant on the left. Turn left and park in the paved lot.

From the Monterey County line, drive 1.5 miles south on Highway 1 to the Ragged Point Inn and Restaurant on the right

Hiking directions: Take the graveled path west (between the snack bar and gift shop) towards the point. Fifty yards ahead is a signed junction at a grassy overlook. The Nature Trail continues straight ahead, circling the blufftop terrace through windswept pine and cypress trees. At the northwest point is a viewing platform. Waterfalls can be seen cascading off the cliffs on both sides of the promontory. Back at the junction, the Cliffside Trail descends down the steps over the cliff's edge past a bench and across a wooden bridge. Switchbacks cut across the edge of the steep cliff to the base of Black Swift Falls at the sandy beach. After enjoying the surroundings, head back up the steep path.

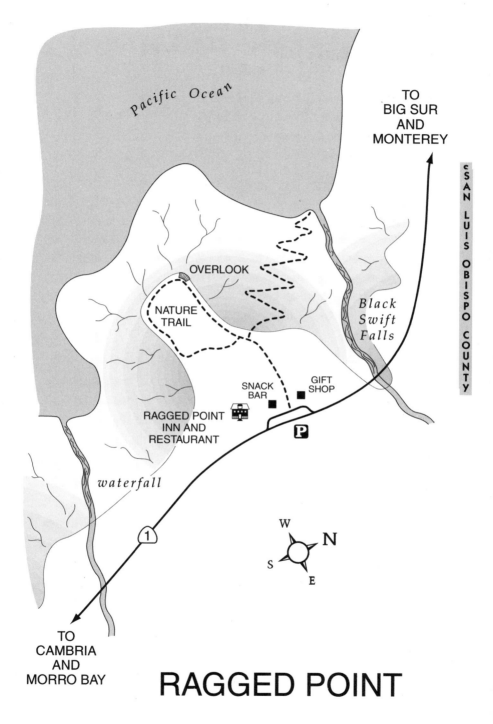

Pacific Ocean

TO
BIG SUR
AND
MONTEREY

SAN LUIS OBISPO COUNTY

OVERLOOK

NATURE
TRAIL

Black
Swift
Falls

SNACK
BAR

GIFT
SHOP

RAGGED POINT
INN AND
RESTAURANT

P

waterfall

1

W

N

S

E

TO
CAMBRIA
AND
MORRO BAY

RAGGED POINT

Hike 26
William R. Hearst State Beach
to San Simeon Point

Hiking distance: 2.5 miles round trip
Hiking time: 1 hour
Elevation gain: 50 feet
Maps: U.S.G.S. San Simeon

Summary of hike: The San Simeon Bay Trail begins at William R. Hearst State Beach along a crescent of white sand. The hike leads to the tip of San Simeon Point, a peninsula extending a half mile into the ocean. The bluff top trails are on the private property of the Hearst Ranch, and although the trails are frequently used, there are no public easements to the point. At the point are beach coves, dramatic rock formations and tidepools. The trail follows the bluffs through a beautiful forest of eucalyptus, pine, cedar and cypress trees. Portions of the bluff top cliffs are unstable and caution is advised.

Driving directions: From Cambria, drive 8 miles north on Highway 1 to William R. Hearst State Beach on the left, across from the turnoff to Hearst Castle. Turn left on San Simeon Road and park 0.2 miles ahead (before crossing the bridge). Pullouts are on both sides of the road by the eucalyptus grove.

From Ragged Point, drive 15 miles south on Highway 1 to the William R. Hearst State Beach on the right.

Hiking directions: Walk through the entrance in the chainlink fence, and follow the path through the eucalyptus grove to the ocean, just west of the pier. Head west along the sand and cross Arroyo del Puerto Creek. Continue towards the forested point. As the beach curves south, take the distinct footpath up to the wooded bluffs. Follow the path through the eucalyptus grove along the edge of the bluffs overlooking the ocean. At the beginning of San Simeon Point, the path joins an unpaved road. Head south across the peninsula to the southeast tip. Various trails lead around the point to endless vistas, beach coves, rock formations and tidepools. The trail continues around the west side of the peninsula through tall cedar and cypress trees, forming a dark shaded tunnel. This is the turn-around spot. Return along the same path.

To hike further, the trail reemerges on the bluffs and descends onto dunes to the beach.

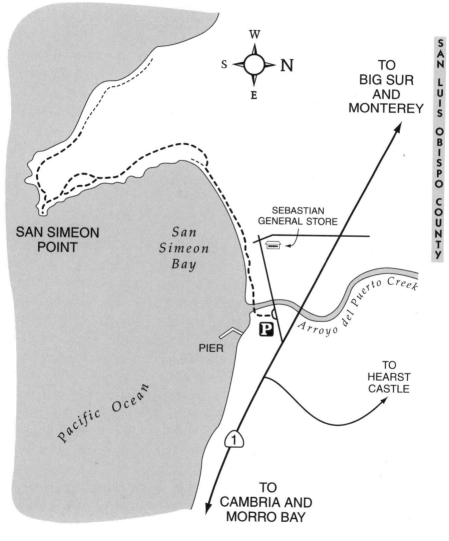

SAN SIMEON POINT

Hike 27
San Simeon Trail
San Simeon State Park

Hiking distance: 4 mile loop
Hiking time: 2 hours
Elevation gain: 200 feet
Maps: U.S.G.S. Cambria

Summary of hike: The San Simeon Trail leads through a diverse landscape of coastal scrub, grassy meadows, wetlands, a Monterey pine forest, a eucalyptus grove and riparian woodlands. This loop hike includes footbridges and boardwalks, interpretive displays, outcroppings, vernal pools of winter rainfall, benches and Whitaker Flats, an 1800s ranch site.

Driving directions: From Highway 1 in Cambria, drive 2 miles north to the San Simeon State Park turnoff on the right. Turn right and park in the Washburn Day Use Area parking lot.

Hiking directions: Follow the wooden boardwalk east to the campground access road and bridge. Bear right on the signed gravel path through the coastal scrub. Cross a footbridge over the wetlands to the edge of the forested hillside. Ascend steps and follow the ridge east through the forest of Monterey pines. At one mile, the path descends down the hillside into Fern Gully, a lush riparian area. Cross the valley floor on Willow Bridge, a long footbridge over the stream and marshland under a canopy of trees. Continue across the grassy slope along the eastern park boundary to a trail fork at the Washburn Campground. The left fork parallels the campground road, returning to the trailhead. Take the right fork across a grassy mesa to a bench and overlook at the Mima Mounds and vernal pools. Bear left, traversing the hillside above San Simeon Creek to a massive forested outcropping. Continue past the formation and head downhill into a eucalyptus grove. Ascend the hillside, joining the trail from the campground. Bear right, parallel to the campground road, back to the trailhead.

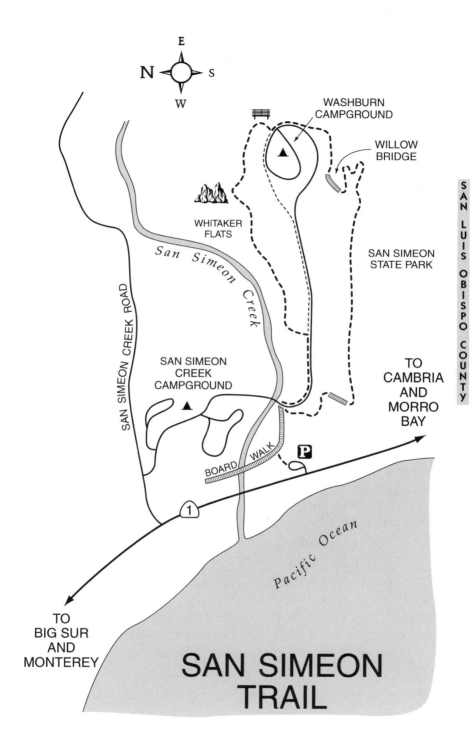

N E S W

WASHBURN
CAMPGROUND

WILLOW
BRIDGE

WHITAKER
FLATS

San Simeon Creek

SAN SIMEON CREEK ROAD

SAN SIMEON
STATE PARK

SAN SIMEON
CREEK
CAMPGROUND

TO
CAMBRIA
AND
MORRO
BAY

BOARD WALK

P

1

SAN LUIS OBISPO COUNTY

Pacific Ocean

TO
BIG SUR
AND
MONTEREY

SAN SIMEON
TRAIL

Hike 28
Moonstone Beach Trail

Hiking distance: 2.5 miles round trip
Hiking time: 1.5 hours
Elevation gain: Level
Maps: U.S.G.S. Cambria

Summary of hike: The Moonstone Beach Trail follows the rocky shoreline at the edge of the windswept ocean cliffs in Cambria. On the 20-foot eroded bluffs along the oceanfront corridor, several staircases lead down to the sandy beach. Along the shore are smooth, translucent, milky white moonstone agates. The trail leads past small coves, rock formations and tidepools to scenic overlooks. There are views up the coast to San Simeon Point and the Piedras Blancas Lighthouse. This is an excellent vantage point to watch migrating gray whales.

Driving directions: From Highway 1 in Cambria, turn west on Windsor Boulevard and a quick right onto Moonstone Beach Drive. Continue 0.3 miles to the Santa Rosa Creek parking lot on the left. Turn left and park.

Hiking directions: The trail begins near the mouth of Santa Rosa Creek on the north end of the parking lot. Head north on the sandstone bluffs overlooking the ocean, parallel to Moonstone Beach Drive. Steps descend to the sandy beach. Return up to the bluffs, crossing small wooden footbridges. At one mile, the old highway bridge spans Leffingwell Creek. Bear left down a ramp to the beach and cross the sand. Ascend the grassy slope to a picnic area and cypress grove at Leffingwell Landing, part of San Simeon State Beach. Cross the parking lot, picking up the trail again on the bluffs, and wind through groves of Monterey pine and cypress. At 1.5 miles is an overlook on the left at the north end of Moonstone Beach Drive. Past the overlook, steps lead down to the beach. Return along the same path.

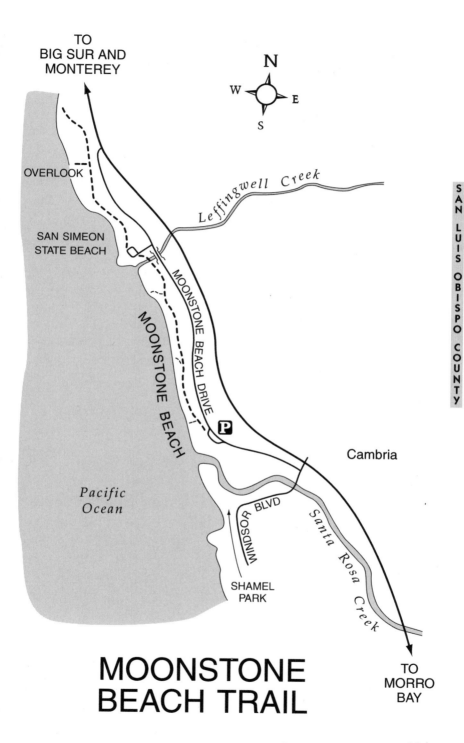

MOONSTONE
BEACH TRAIL

Hike 29
East West Ranch Bluff Trail

Hiking distance: 2 miles round trip
Hiking time: 1 hour
Elevation gain: Level
Maps: U.S.G.S. Cambria

Summary of hike: The East West Ranch Bluff Trail in Cambria follows the edge of the eroded bluffs above the ocean. The rocky shore and tidepools can be seen below. There are two bridge crossings, a handcrafted wooden shelter and several unique benches. The one-mile long trail crosses a private ranch from Windsor Boulevard in the south to Windsor Boulevard in the north. There is no beach access on the trail, but the views are fantastic.

Driving directions: From Highway 1 in Cambria, head south on Burton Drive. Go 0.3 miles to Ardath Drive and turn right. Drive 0.7 miles to Madison Street and bear right. Continue 0.2 miles to Orlando Drive and turn left. Go 0.2 miles to Windsor Boulevard and turn right. Park one block ahead at the end of the road.

Hiking directions: Head north through the trailhead gate and cross the flat grassy bluffs that overlook the jagged shoreline, tidepools and the ocean. Cross the wooden footbridge over a stream. The trail curves along the edge of the eroded bluffs. Cross a second bridge, then head past benches and a wooden shelter. The trail ends by a fenceline at the southern edge of a residential neighborhood. Return along the same trail.

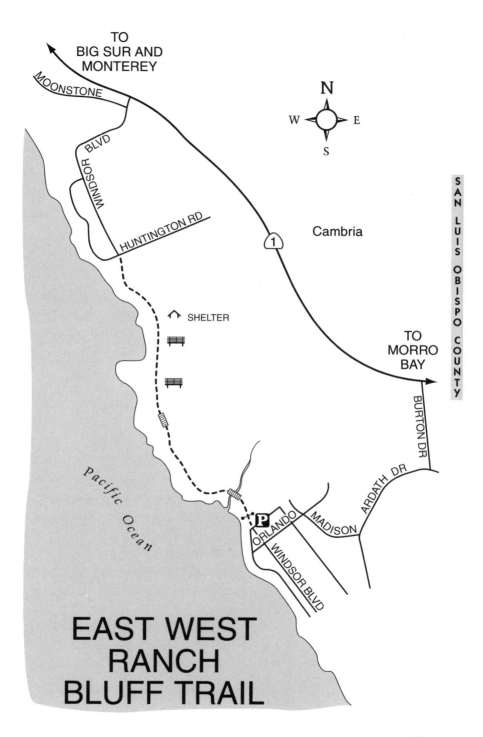

TO
BIG SUR AND
MONTEREY

MOONSTONE

BLVD

WINDSOR

HUNTINGTON RD

N

W — E

S

Cambria

1

SHELTER

TO
MORRO
BAY

BURTON DR

ARDATH DR

Pacific Ocean

P

ORLANDO

MADISON

WINDSOR BLVD

SAN LUIS OBISPO COUNTY

EAST WEST RANCH BLUFF TRAIL

Hike 30
Cloisters Wetland to Morro Rock

Hiking distance: 3.5 miles round trip
Hiking time: 1.5 hours
Elevation gain: Level
Maps: U.S.G.S. Morro Bay North and Morro Bay South

Summary of hike: The Cloisters Wetland is a 2.6-acre wildlife habitat with a freshwater lagoon. A trail with interpretive signs circles the lagoon. The hike crosses Morro Strand State Beach to Morro Rock, a dome-shaped volcanic plug rising from the ocean at the mouth of the harbor. This ancient 578-foot monolithic outcropping is a wildlife preserve.

Driving directions: From Highway 1 in Morro Bay, head 2 miles north to San Jacinto Street and turn left. Drive to the first street and turn left again on Coral Avenue. Continue 0.3 miles and park in the Cloisters Community Park parking lot on the right.

Hiking directions: Take the paved path through the developed park along the south side of the lagoon. At the dunes is a junction. The right fork circles the Cloisters Wetland, a freshwater lagoon. Bear left and follow the path between the dunes and the park meadow towards the prominent Morro Rock. The trail curves through the dunes, crossing a wooden footbridge. Bear right and walk parallel to a row of pine trees to the end of the boardwalk at the sandy beach. Follow the shoreline of Morro Strand State Beach directly towards Morro Rock. Cross the sand isthmus to the base of the rock. Walk across the parking area and follow Coleman Drive (the paved road) clockwise around the perimeter of Morro Rock along the edge of the bay. At the west end of the rock is a sandy beach and breakwater at the entrance to the bay. Return along the same route.

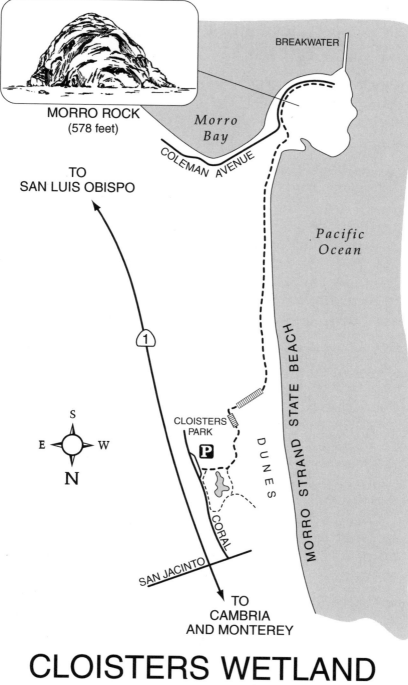

MORRO ROCK
(578 feet)

BREAKWATER

Morro Bay

COLEMAN AVENUE

TO
SAN LUIS OBISPO

Pacific Ocean

1

S

E ⊕ W

N

CLOISTERS PARK

P

MORRO STRAND STATE BEACH

D U N E S

CORAL

SAN JACINTO

TO
CAMBRIA
AND MONTEREY

CLOISTERS WETLAND

Hike 31
Black Hill
Morro Bay State Park

Hiking distance: 0.6—2.6 miles round trip
Hiking time: 30 minutes—1.5 hours
Elevation gain: 180—540 feet
Maps: U.S.G.S. Morro Bay South

Summary of hike: Black Hill (also known an Black Mountain) is an ancient 661-foot volcanic peak in Morro Bay State Park. There is a short easy trail to the rocky summit and a longer forested route. The longer route climbs through the shade of a eucalyptus forest, an oak woodland and Monterey pine groves. From the rocky summit are panoramic views of Morro Bay and the estuary, Estero Point, Cayucos, Chorro Valley, and the near-by morros of Cerro Cabrillo and Hollister Peak. The ocean views span from Montaña de Oro to San Simeon.

Driving directions: From Highway 101 south of San Luis Obispo, take the Los Osos Valley Road exit, and head 9.6 miles west to South Bay Road. Turn right and continue 3.2 miles to State Park Road and turn left.

From Highway 1 in Morro Bay, head 0.8 miles south on South Bay Boulevard to State Park Road and turn right.

FOR THE LONG HIKE, bear right 0.1 mile ahead at a road fork and head up Park View Drive for 0.3 miles to a parking pullout on the left.

FOR THE SHORT HIKE, bear right 0.1 mile ahead at a road fork and head 0.6 miles up Park View Drive to the unsigned Black Mountain Road and turn right. Continue 0.7 miles through the golf course to the trailhead parking area at the end of the road.

Hiking directions: For the long hike, walk 100 yards up the road to the trail on the right with the "no bikes" sign. Head north across a meadow, dropping into a ravine to a T-junction. Bear left through a eucalyptus grove past an intersecting trail on the right. A short distance ahead is a third junction. Bear right, gaining elevation through an oak woodland. At one mile, loop around the right side of a cement water tank to the upper trail-head parking lot. This is where the short hike begins. Head northeast up several switchbacks to the summit. After marveling at the views, return by retracing your steps.

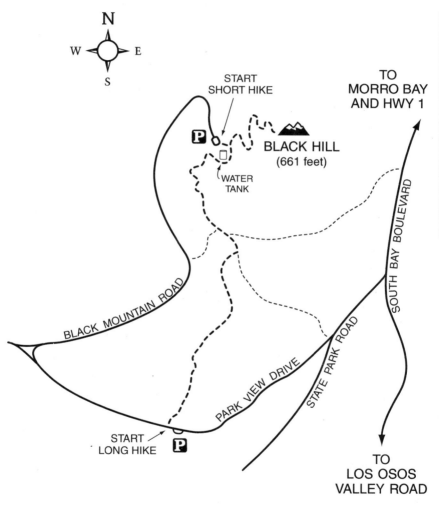

BLACK HILL

Hike 32
Portola Point
Morro Bay State Park

Hiking distance: 2 miles round trip
Hiking time: 1 hour
Elevation gain: 320 feet
Maps: U.S.G.S. Morro Bay South
       The Mountain Biking Map for San Luis Obispo

Summary of hike: Portola Hill is a 329-foot rounded volcanic hill on the east side of Morro Bay State Park. A spur trail leads up to Portola Point, offering sweeping views of the surrounding morros and the Morro Bay area, one of the most vital and productive bird habitats in the country. The hike follows the Quarry and Live Oak Trails across rolling native grassland, looping around the base of Portola Hill.

Driving directions: From Highway 101 south of San Luis Obispo, take the Los Osos Valley Road exit, and head 9.6 miles west to South Bay Road. Turn right and continue 2.6 miles to the trailhead parking lot on the right.

From Highway 1 in Morro Bay, head 1.4 miles south on South Bay Boulevard to the trailhead parking lot on the left.

Hiking directions: Take the signed Quarry Trail uphill through the sage scrub. Head east along the south facing slopes of Cerro Cabrillo to a signed junction at 0.5 miles. Take the Live Oak Trail to the right, descending across a grassy meadow towards Portola Hill. Near the base of the hill is a signed trail fork. Bear right on the Portola Trail, and ascend the hill past an oak grove. Switchbacks lead up to a trail split, circling the point to various overlooks and a resting bench. Complete the loop and return to the Live Oak Trail. Go right and descend into the draw between Portola Hill and Hill 811. At 1.5 miles is a signed trail split. Bear right, contouring around Portola Hill on the Live Oak Trail. Return to the parking lot.

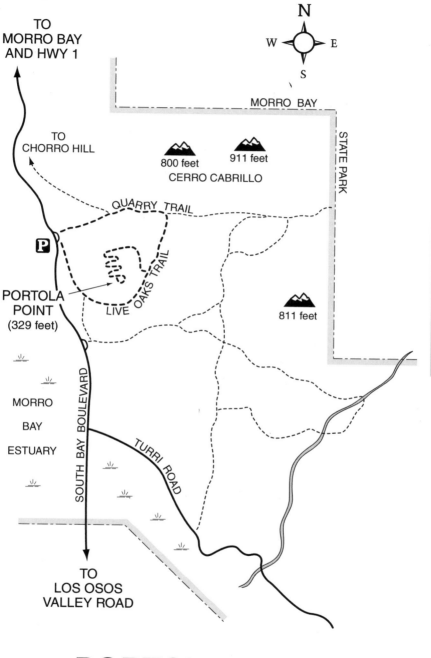

TO
MORRO BAY
AND HWY 1

N
W E
S

MORRO BAY

TO
CHORRO HILL

STATE PARK

800 feet 911 feet
CERRO CABRILLO

QUARRY TRAIL

P

811 feet

PORTOLA
POINT
(329 feet)

LIVE OAKS TRAIL

SAN LUIS OBISPO COUNTY

MORRO

BAY

ESTUARY

SOUTH BAY BOULEVARD

TURRI ROAD

TO
LOS OSOS
VALLEY ROAD

PORTOLA POINT

Hike 33
Quarry and Park Ridge Loop Trail
Morro Bay State Park

Hiking distance: 2.5 miles round trip
Hiking time: 1 hour
Elevation gain: 350 feet
Maps: U.S.G.S. Morro Bay South
        The Mountain Biking Map for San Luis Obispo

Summary of hike: The Quarry and Park Ridge Trails are on the east side of Morro Bay State Park under the shadow of Cerro Cabrillo, a 911-foot double-peaked ridge. The Quarry Trail skirts the southern flank of Cerro Cabrillo past the rubble piles of an abandoned quarry site used for road construction in 1959. The Park Ridge Trail is an old farm road that crosses the rolling grasslands.

Driving directions: From Highway 101 south of San Luis Obispo, take the Los Osos Valley Road exit, and head 9.6 miles west to South Bay Road. Turn right and continue 2.6 miles to the trailhead parking lot on the right.
    From Highway 1 in Morro Bay, head 1.4 miles south on South Bay Boulevard to the trailhead parking lot on the left.

Hiking directions: Take the signed Quarry Trail toward the foot of Cerro Cabrillo. The trail parallels the base of the mountain, passing the quarry site on the left. Continue past the Live Oak Trail on the right to a junction at 0.9 miles with the Park Ridge Trail on the right. Stay on the Quarry Trail, heading east to the signed junction with the Canet Trail on the right. The Quarry Trail ends 0.2 miles ahead at the fenced park boundary. Take the Canet Trail south, crossing the rolling hill to a saddle and a junction. Bear left on the Park Ridge Trail, and head downhill to a trail split with the Chumash Trail. Veer right and stay right again at a junction with the Crespi Trail. Cross a small bridge, returning to a gate near South Bay Road. Bear right (north) on the Live Oak Trail back to the parking lot.

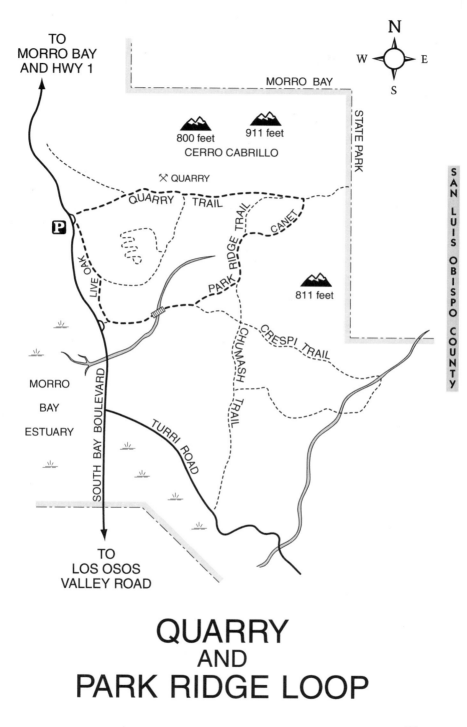

QUARRY
AND
PARK RIDGE LOOP

Hike 34
Elfin Forest Natural Area

Hiking distance: 1.5 miles round trip
Hiking time: 1 hour
Elevation gain: 100 feet
Maps: U.S.G.S. Morro Bay South

Summary of hike: The Elfin Forest Natural Area is a 92-acre refuge at the eastern shore of Morro Bay, abutting the estuary. A mile of wooden walkways with viewing platforms and over-looks form an oval loop around the forest. The area includes a salt marsh, coastal dune scrub, morro manzanita, riparian wood-land and dense stands of dwarfed 500-year-old pygmy oaks. The gnarled, windswept oaks have room-like openings and are draped with moss and lichens.

Driving directions: From Highway 101 south of San Luis Obispo, take the Los Osos Valley Road exit, and head 9.6 miles west to South Bay Road. Turn right and continue 1.4 miles to Santa Ysabel Avenue on the left. Turn left and drive to 16th Street. Turn right and park at the end of the block.

From Highway 1 in Morro Bay, head 2.7 miles south on South Bay Boulevard to Santa Ysabel Avenue. Turn right and follow the directions above.

Hiking directions: Head north at the end of 16th Street on the wooden boardwalk. Walk through the dense sage scrub to the ridge overlooking the Morro Bay estuary. Bear left (west), following the Ridge Trail boardwalk to an overlook at the west end. A sandy path returns to 11th and 13th Streets. From the overlook, return east 150 yards to a junction and bear left. Descend to the Celestial Meadow Trail. The left fork leads to another overlook platform at the edge of the estuary. The right fork heads uphill to a junction with the Ridge Trail. Here the left fork leads to a third viewing platform. The right fork completes the loop on the ridge by 16th Street.

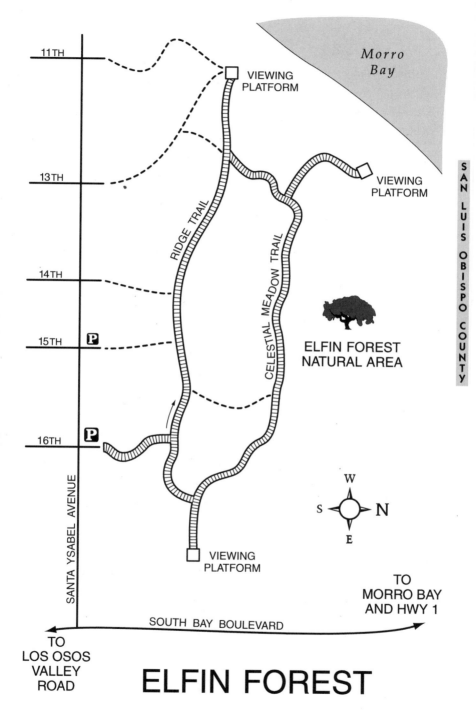

11TH

VIEWING
PLATFORM

*Morro
Bay*

13TH

VIEWING
PLATFORM

RIDGE TRAIL

CELESTIAL MEADOW TRAIL

S A N   L U I S   O B I S P O   C O U N T Y

14TH

ELFIN FOREST
NATURAL AREA

15TH **P**

16TH **P**

SANTA YSABEL AVENUE

W

S N

E

VIEWING
PLATFORM

TO
MORRO BAY
AND HWY 1

SOUTH BAY BOULEVARD

TO
LOS OSOS
VALLEY
ROAD

ELFIN FOREST

Hike 35
Sweet Springs Nature Preserve

Hiking distance: 0.5 to 1 mile round trip
Hiking time: 30 minutes
Elevation gain: Level
Maps: U.S.G.S. Morro Bay South

Summary of hike: Sweet Springs Nature Preserve is a 24-acre wetland sanctuary for nesting and migrating birds on the southeast shore of Morro Bay. There are two serene freshwater ponds, a saltwater marsh at the bay, Monterey cypress and eucalyptus groves. The eucalyptus groves are home to monarch butterflies during the winter months. The preserve is managed by the Morro Coast Audubon Society

Driving directions: From Highway 101 south of San Luis Obispo, take the Los Osos Valley Road exit, and head 10.1 miles west to 9th Street (0.5 miles past South Bay Boulevard). Turn right and drive 0.6 miles to Ramona Avenue, curving to the left. Continue 0.5 miles to the nature preserve on the right. Park along the road.

From Highway 1 in Morro Bay, head 4 miles south on South Bay Boulevard to Los Osos Valley Road and turn right. Continue 0.5 miles to 9th Street and turn right. Follow directions above.

Hiking directions: From the preserve entrance gate, walk past the trail sign and cross a wooden footbridge over the pond. Bear left to a second wooden bridge. Towards the right is a maze of waterways winding through the estuary. After crossing the bridge, the trail weaves through a eucalyptus grove. At the west end of the preserve is a junction. The left fork returns to the road at Broderson Street. The right fork leads to an overlook of the bay and marshy tidelands. Morro Rock can be seen at the north end of the bay. Return to the first bridge. Bear to the left, heading east alongside the pond. The trail loops back through another eucalyptus grove and returns to the park entrance.

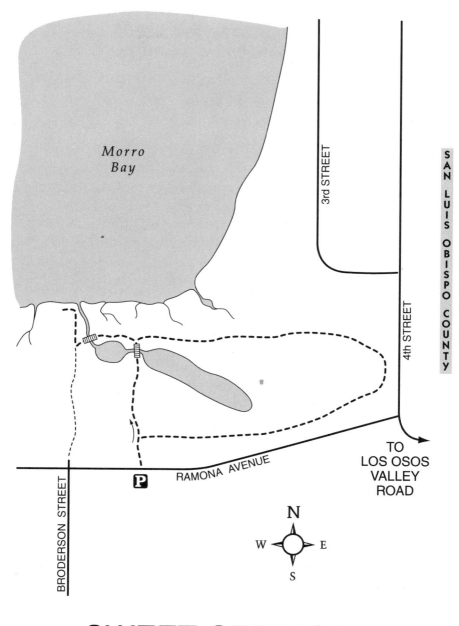

Morro Bay

3rd STREET

4th STREET

TO
LOS OSOS
VALLEY
ROAD

RAMONA AVENUE

P

BRODERSON STREET

N
W E
S

SWEET SPRINGS NATURE PRESERVE

Hike 36
Morro Bay Sand Spit
Montaña de Oro State Park

Hiking distance: 8 to 9.5 miles round trip
Hiking time: 3 to 5 hours
Elevation gain: 50 feet
Maps: U.S.G.S. Morro Bay South
Montaña de Oro State Park map

Summary of hike: The Morro Bay Sand Spit is three-mile long narrow vein of land that separates Morro Bay and the estuary from the waters of Estero Bay and the Pacific Ocean. A fragile 80-foot sand dune ridge, stabilized by scrubs, grasses and succulents, runs the length of this natural preserve. Along the dunes are ancient Chumash Indian shell mounds. This hike follows the sand spit along the ocean side of the dunes.

Driving directions: From Highway 101 south of San Luis Obispo, take the Los Osos Valley Road exit, and head 12.1 miles west to the Montaña de Oro State Park entrance. Los Osos Valley Road becomes Pecho Valley Road en route. Continue 0.8 miles to Sand Spit Road and turn right. Drive 0.5 miles to the parking lot at the end of the road.

Hiking directions: Take the lined path past the information boards and head west across the scrub-covered sand dunes. The path reaches the ocean at 0.2 miles. Head north along the hard-packed sand close to the shoreline for easier walking. The coastline has an abundance of sea shells. At 4 miles is the first of two breakwaters guarding the bay entrance. Morro Rock, a 578-foot volcanic rock, dominates the landscape. This is a good turnaround spot. To add an additional 1.5 miles to the hike, continue following the shoreline to a second breakwater. Curve east towards Morro Bay, and follow the bay south about one mile. The trail curves west, crossing the soft sands of the dunes back to the ocean.

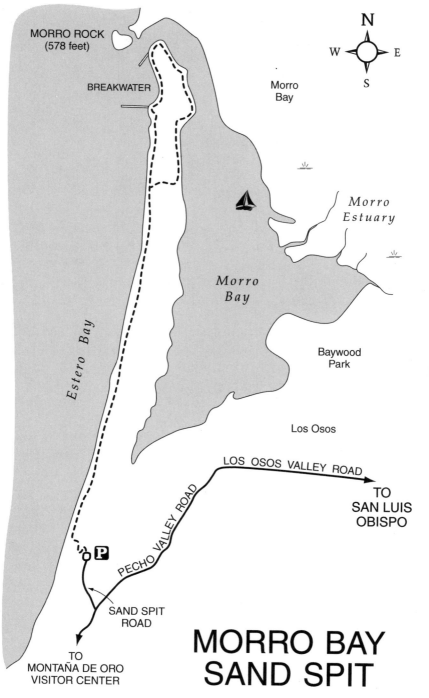

MORRO ROCK
(578 feet)

BREAKWATER

Morro
Bay

*Morro
Estuary*

*Morro
Bay*

Estero Bay

Baywood
Park

Los Osos

LOS OSOS VALLEY ROAD

**TO
SAN LUIS
OBISPO**

PECHO VALLEY ROAD

P

SAND SPIT
ROAD

TO
MONTAÑA DE ORO
VISITOR CENTER

N
W   E
S

MORRO BAY
SAND SPIT

Hike 37
Reservoir Flats Trail
Montaña de Oro State Park

Hiking distance: 2.1 mile loop
Hiking time: 1 hour
Elevation gain: 250 feet
Maps: U.S.G.S. Morro Bay South
Montaña de Oro State Park map

Summary of hike: The Reservoir Flats Trail follows a creekside canyon parallel to Islay Creek. Ferns and moss carpet the lush canyon, willows line the creek, and lichen streamers hang from the branches of the trees. After leaving the canyon, the trail reaches a ridge along the grassy hillside to the former reservoir site. From the ridge are views of Islay Canyon, the bluffs, Spooner's Cove and the Pacific Ocean.

Driving directions: From Highway 101 south of San Luis Obispo, take the Los Osos Valley Road exit, and head 12.1 miles west to the Montaña de Oro State Park entrance. Los Osos Valley Road becomes Pecho Valley Road en route. Continue 2.6 miles to the visitor center on the left and park.

Hiking directions: From the visitor center, walk east up the Islay Creek Campground road 0.4 miles to the Reservoir Flats Trail by campsite 40. Continue east on the footpath up the lush drainage, and traverse the hillside above the meandering Islay Creek. At 1.1 mile is a junction. The left fork is a short detour to the creek. Return and bear left, heading out of the shady canyon to an overlook. Descend from the ridge to Reservoir Flats, an open grassy bowl. Stay to the right at the signed Oats Peak Trail. Cross the sage-scrub hill and descend back to the visitor center.

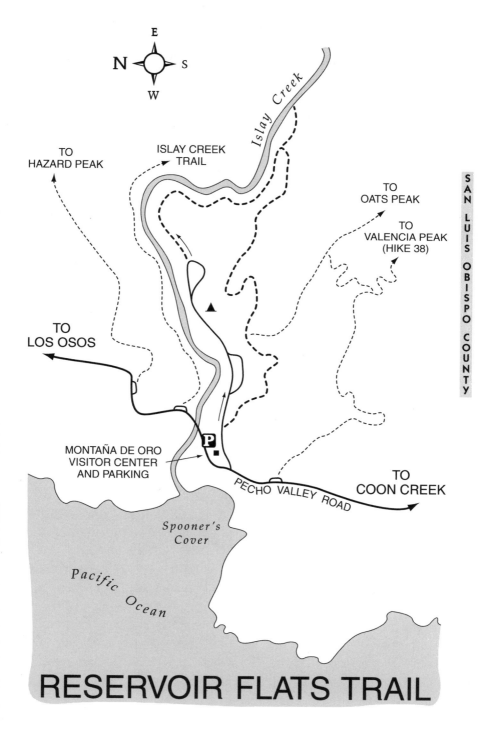

RESERVOIR FLATS TRAIL

Hike 38
Valencia Peak Trail
Montaña de Oro State Park

Hiking distance: 4 miles round trip
Hiking time: 2 hours
Elevation gain: 1,150 feet
Maps: U.S.G.S. Morro Bay South
Montaña de Oro State Park map

Summary of hike: Valencia Peak, at 1,347 feet, has spectacular 360-degree views of Montaña de Oro, Morro Bay, Los Osos Valley and the rugged coastline from Point Sal to Piedras Blancas. The chain of morros leading to San Luis Obispo are in view. The trail crosses grasslands and straddles a ridge between two canyons before climbing directly up to the coastal peak.

Driving directions: From Highway 101 south of San Luis Obispo, take the Los Osos Valley Road exit, and head 12.1 miles west to the Montaña de Oro State Park entrance. Los Osos Valley Road becomes Pecho Valley Road en route. Continue 2.6 miles to the visitor center on the left. The trailhead parking area is on the left on Pecho Valley Road, a hundred yards past the visitor center.

Hiking directions: Hike east across the sage-covered flat on the signed trail. Head toward the base of the mountain, passing the Rattlesnake Flats Trail on the right. As the trail begins to climb, views of the scenic coastal plain open up. Switchbacks lead up to the first ridge above Spooner's Cove and the bluffs. Cross the grassy flat, in full view of Valencia Peak, to a junction at the base of the cone-shaped mountain. The left fork leads to the Oats Peak Trail. Take the right fork, climbing the edge of the mountain to a narrow ridge. Follow the ridge east up two steep sections with loose shale. At the base of the final ascent is another junction with the Oaks Peak Trail—stay to the right. Continue uphill, reaching the summit at two miles. After savoring the views, return along the same route.

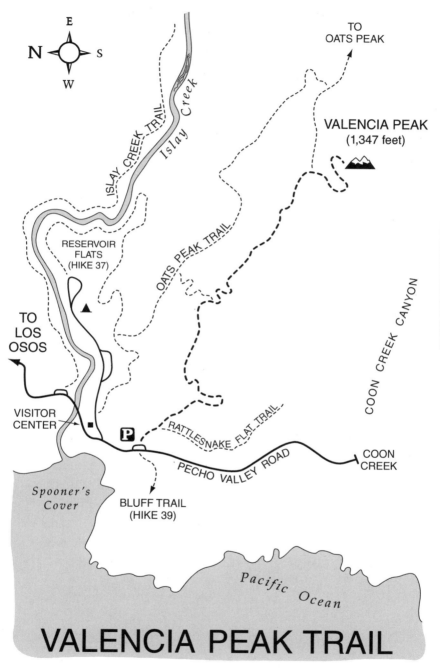

VALENCIA PEAK TRAIL

Hike 39
Bluff Trail
Montaña de Oro State Park

Hiking distance: 3.4 miles round trip
Hiking time: 1.5 hours
Elevation gain: Level
Maps: U.S.G.S. Morro Bay South
Montaña de Oro State Park map

Summary of hike: The Bluff Trail is an easy hike along one of the premier locations on the central California coastline. The trail snakes along the contours of a rugged network of eroding sandstone bluffs on a grassy marine terrace. Land extensions jut out into the ocean like fingers. There are hidden coves, sea caves, arches, sandy beaches, reefs, offshore outcroppings, clear tidepools, crashing surf, and basking seals and otters.

Driving directions: From Highway 101 south of San Luis Obispo, take the Los Osos Valley Road exit, and head 12.1 miles west to the Montaña de Oro State Park entrance. Los Osos Valley Road becomes Pecho Valley Road en route. Drive 2.6 miles to the visitor center on the left. The trailhead parking area is on the right on Pecho Valley Road, a hundred yards past the visitor center.

Hiking directions: Head west on the wide trail, and cross a wooden bridge to a trail fork. Take the right branch, following the cliff's edge along Spooner's Cove. Spur trails intersect the main trail throughout the hike, leading back to the road. The main path generally follows the cliff's edge, passing coves and rocky reefs. At Corallina Cove, the trail curves inland, crosses a foot-bridge over a narrow ravine, and returns to the ocean cliffs. Continue south past Quarry Cove, another sandy beach with tidepools. At 1.7 miles, is Grotto Rock, a prominent castle-shaped rock with caves near the PG&E fenceline. This is the turnaround spot. The trail leaves the coastline here and heads east to Pecho Valley Road. To return, retrace your steps.

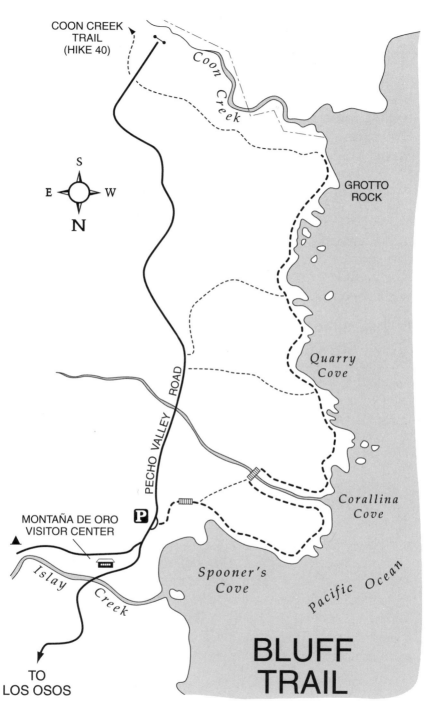

COON CREEK
TRAIL
(HIKE 40)

Coon Creek

GROTTO
ROCK

S

E ✦ W

N

*Quarry
Cove*

PECHO VALLEY ROAD

*Corallina
Cove*

MONTAÑA DE ORO
VISITOR CENTER

P

Islay

Creek

*Spooner's
Cove*

Pacific Ocean

BLUFF
TRAIL

TO
LOS OSOS

Hike 40
Coon Creek Trail
Montaña de Oro State Park

Hiking distance: 5 miles round trip
Hiking time: 2.5 hours
Elevation gain: 200 feet
Maps: U.S.G.S. Morro Bay South and Port San Luis
Montaña de Oro State Park map

Summary of hike: The Coon Creek Trail heads up Coon Creek Canyon alongside the winding watercourse of the year-round stream. The trail crosses six bridges over the creek through the shade of the lush riparian corridor. Willows, maples, cottonwoods, oaks, cedars and cypress grow in the canyon with Spanish moss hanging from the branches.

Driving directions: From Highway 101 south of San Luis Obispo, take the Los Osos Valley Road exit, and head 12.1 miles west to the Montaña de Oro State Park entrance. Los Osos Valley Road becomes Pecho Valley Road en route. Continue 3.9 miles to the trailhead parking area on the left at the end of the road. It is 1.2 miles past the visitor center.

Hiking directions: Hike east past the trail sign and over a small ridge to a ravine. Bear right down wide steps, and follow the path along a fenceline to Coon Creek at 0.3 miles. Head up the canyon through the forest along the north side of the creek. Cross the first of six bridges over the creek past beautiful rock outcroppings. At 1.2 miles, the trail rises to an overlook of Coon Creek Canyon at a signed trail junction with the Rattlesnake Flats Trail on the left. Continue straight ahead up the shady canyon, and cross several more bridges. There is a junction on the left with the Oats Peak Trail at 2.4 miles. Continue a short distance ahead to the trail's end in a grove of old cedars and large oaks at an old cabin site. Return by retracing your steps.

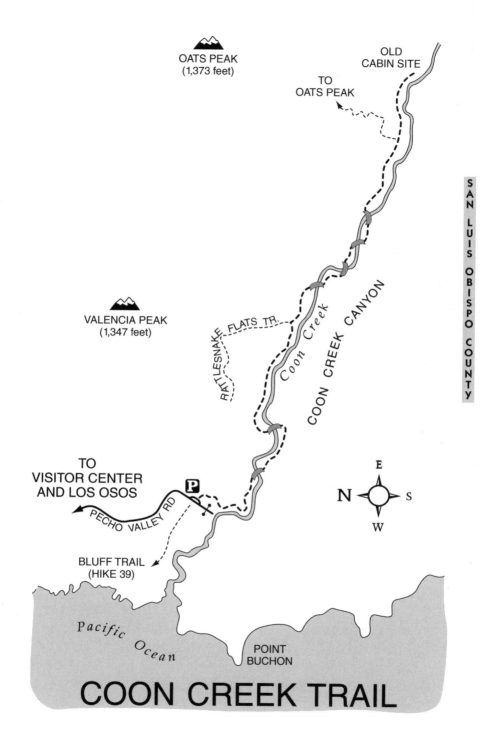

OATS PEAK
(1,373 feet)

OLD
CABIN SITE

TO
OATS PEAK

SAN LUIS OBISPO COUNTY

VALENCIA PEAK
(1,347 feet)

RATTLESNAKE FLATS TR.

Coon Creek

COON CREEK CANYON

TO
VISITOR CENTER
AND LOS OSOS

P

PECHO VALLEY RD

E

N — S

W

BLUFF TRAIL
(HIKE 39)

Pacific Ocean

POINT
BUCHON

COON CREEK TRAIL

Hike 41
Pecho Coast Trail
Free docent-led hike on PG&E land
Reservations required: (805) 541-8735

Hiking distance: 3.5—7.4 miles round trip
Hiking time: 4 hours—7 hours
Elevation gain: 440 feet
Maps: U.S.G.S. Port San Luis

Summary of hike: The Pecho Coast Trail curves around the northern point of San Luis Obispo Bay from Port San Luis towards Moñtana de Oro State Park. There are two docent-led hikes across the privately owned PG&E land. Both hikes follow the steep cliffs to Point San Luis and the Port San Luis Lighthouse, a two-story Victorian redwood structure built in 1890. It is a great spot for watching the annual migration of the gray whales. The longer hike continues across the coastal bluffs and pastureland to an oak grove in Rattlesnake Canyon.

Driving directions: From Highway 101 in Pismo Beach, take the Avila Beach Drive exit. Head 4.2 miles west, passing the town of Avila, to the PG&E Diablo Canyon Power Plant entrance on the right at Port San Luis Harbor. Park in the wide area on the left, across the road from the PG&E entrance gate.

Hiking directions: Naturalists will lead the hike, providing geological, botanical and historical details. Begin by walking up the steps past a locked gate west of the PG&E station. Ascend the hillside overlooking the bay and three piers. Bear left on the lighthouse road to the Pecho Coast Trail, and take the footpath left. Descend the hillside towards the ocean. Follow the contour of the mountains on a cliffside trail 200 feet above the ocean. The trail passes Smith Island and Whaler's Island. Continue around the point, rejoining the paved road to the lighthouse.

The longer hike continues past the lighthouse, crossing the coastal terrace and grasslands to an oak woodland in Rattlesnake Canyon for lunch. Return by retracing your steps.

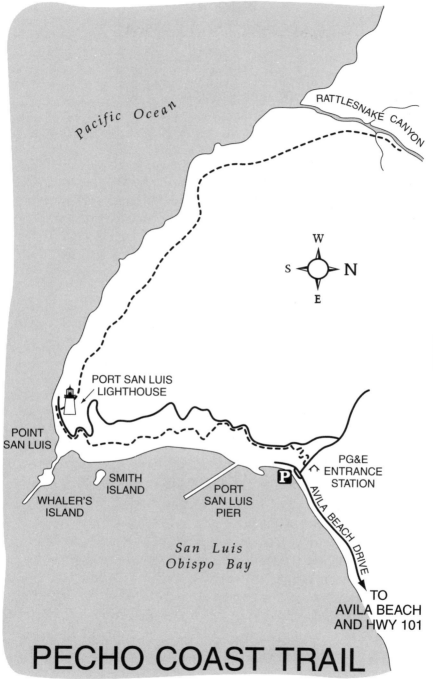

Pacific Ocean

RATTLESNAKE CANYON

W N S E

PORT SAN LUIS
LIGHTHOUSE

POINT
SAN LUIS

SMITH
ISLAND

WHALER'S
ISLAND

PORT
SAN LUIS
PIER

P

PG&E
ENTRANCE
STATION

AVILA BEACH DRIVE

San Luis
Obispo Bay

TO
AVILA BEACH
AND HWY 101

PECHO COAST TRAIL

Hike 42
Cave Landing and Pirate's Cove

Hiking distance: 2 miles round trip
Hiking time: 1 hour
Elevation gain: 120 feet
Maps: U.S.G.S. Pismo Beach
      The Thomas Guide—San Luis Obispo County

Summary of hike: Cave Landing, also known as Mallagh Landing, is a spectacular rocky promontory that juts out 150 feet into the bay, forming a natural pier. This beautiful formation has caves and coves, including an arch carved through the cliffs near the headland point. From the point are great views of the steep, chiseled cliffs along the rugged coastline. Pirate's Cove, a crescent-shaped, clothing-optional beach, sits at the base of the hundred-foot cliffs.

Driving directions: From Highway 101 in Pismo Beach, exit on Avila Beach Drive. Head 2 miles west to Cave Landing Road and turn left. Continue 0.5 miles to the trailhead parking lot on the right at the end of the road.

Hiking directions: The trail heads southeast towards the rocky point overlooking the Shell Beach and Pismo Beach coastline. At 20 yards is a junction. Bear left to a trail split 0.2 miles ahead. The left fork descends to Pirate's Cove. Before descending, take the right fork to another trail split. To the right is a natural arch cave leading to an overlook. To the left is another overlook at the edge of the cliffs. Return to the junction and bear right, curving gently down the cliffs to Pirate's Cove. Continue along the sandy beach beneath the cliffs. Return along the same path.

For an additional 0.6-mile hike, take the wide path heading west at the opposite end of the trailhead parking area. The trail leads down to a flat, grassy plateau. From the plateau, a path follows the cliff's edge to the left. Caves can be seen along the base of the cliffs. Return the way you came.

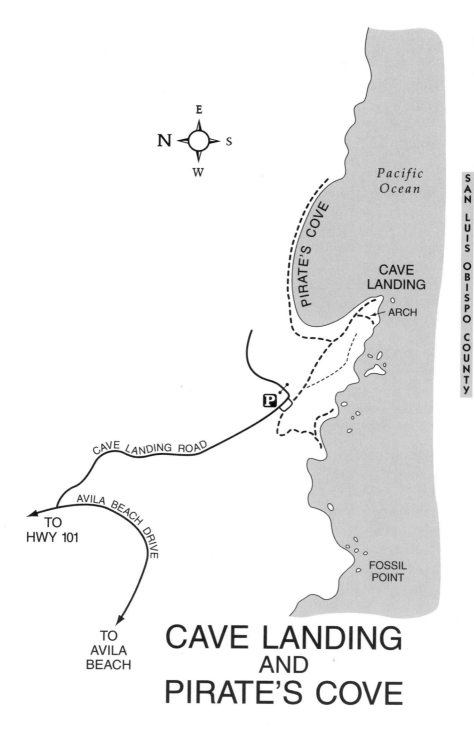

N E S W

Pacific
Ocean

PIRATE'S COVE

CAVE
LANDING

o
ARCH

P

CAVE LANDING ROAD

AVILA BEACH DRIVE

TO
HWY 101

TO
AVILA
BEACH

SAN LUIS OBISPO COUNTY

FOSSIL
POINT

CAVE LANDING
AND
PIRATE'S COVE

Hike 43
Bob Jones City to the Sea Bike Trail

Hiking distance: 5.6 miles round trip
Hiking time: 2.5 hour
Elevation gain: 150 feet
Maps: U.S.G.S. Pismo Beach
        The Thomas Guide—San Luis Obispo County

Summary of hike: The Bob Jones City to the Sea Bike Trail (originally known as the Avila Valley Bike Trail) follows the old Pacific Coast Railroad right-of-way. It is used as a hiking, jogging and biking route. The paved trail winds through the forested valley alongside San Luis Obispo Creek towards Avila Beach. From the trail are views of bridges spanning the wide creek, the Avila Beach Golf Course, the town of Avila and the Pacific Ocean.

Driving directions: From Highway 101 in Pismo Beach, exit on Avila Beach Drive. Head west 0.3 miles to Ontario Road at Avila Hot Springs Spa. Turn right and continue 0.3 miles, crossing the bridge over San Luis Obispo Creek, to the trailhead parking lot on the right.

Hiking directions: Cross Ontario Road and pick up the signed trail heading west. The trail immediately enters a lush forest parallel to San Luis Obispo Creek. Although you are near the creek, the dense foliage makes access to the creek nearly impossible. At 0.7 miles, cross a bridge over See Canyon Creek, and then cross San Luis Bay Drive at one mile. Continue past Avila Bay Club on the right and the creek on the left to the trail's end at Blue Heron Drive. Bear left on the private road, staying close to the creek. The road curves around the hillside overlooking the creek, bridges and golf course. At the first bridge spanning the creek is a junction. The left fork heads across the bridge to Avila Beach Drive. The right fork continues to the golf course entrance by Mulligans Restaurant. Both paths lead to Avila Beach. To return, take the same trail back.

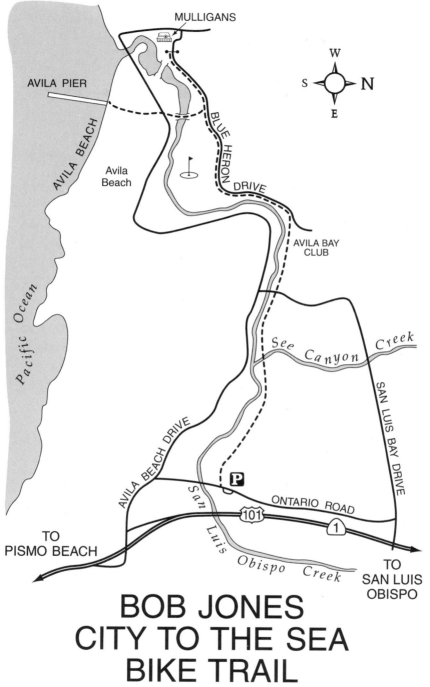

MULLIGANS

AVILA PIER

AVILA BEACH

Avila
Beach

BLUE HERON DRIVE

Pacific Ocean

AVILA BAY
CLUB

See Canyon Creek

AVILA BEACH DRIVE

San Luis Obispo Creek

SAN LUIS BAY DRIVE

P

ONTARIO ROAD

101

1

TO
PISMO BEACH

TO
SAN LUIS
OBISPO

BOB JONES
CITY TO THE SEA
BIKE TRAIL

Hike 44
Guiton Trail
Oceano Lagoon

Hiking distance: 1.5 mile loop
Hiking time: 1 hour
Elevation gain: Level
Maps: U.S.G.S. Oceano
Pismo State Beach map

Summary of hike: The Guiton Trail circles the Oceano Lagoon, a tranquil freshwater lagoon. The trail is named for Harold E. Guiton who donated five acres of lagoon property to the state parks in the mid-1930s. The lagoon is a popular spot for fishing, canoeing and bird watching. The lush riparian habitat creates a secluded pastoral stroll through a forested canopy of Monterey pines, eucalyptus and willows.

Driving directions: From Highway 101 in Pismo Beach, take the Pismo Beach/Highway 1 South exit. Take Highway 1 through the town of Pismo Beach (Dolliver Street, which becomes Pacific Boulevard) for 3 miles to Pier Avenue. Turn right and drive 0.2 miles to the Oceano Campground. Turn right into the campground and park by the nature center on the right.

Hiking directions: Pick up the signed footpath by the lagoon, east of the nature center. Bear left, skirting the eastern edge of the campground along the water's edge. Follow the forested shoreline north, joining a paved path with benches. Curve around the northwest tip of the lagoon where the paved path ends. Loop around the perimeter of the grassy peninsula on the footpath. At the north tip of the lagoon, the trail meets a road at the Parks and Recreation buildings. Bear right, picking up the trail on the east side of the lagoon. Head south through the lush native forest, crossing several footbridges over streams and channels. The trail ends at the bridge on Pier Avenue. Cross the bridge over the lagoon, returning to the nature center.

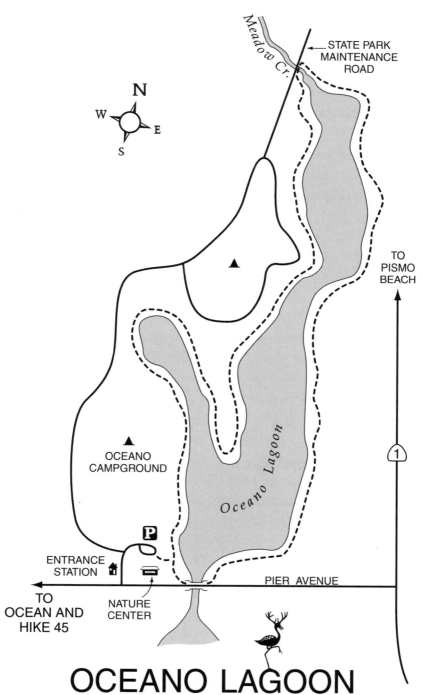

State Park Maintenance Road

Meadow Cr.

N
W   E
S

TO PISMO BEACH

SAN LUIS OBISPO COUNTY

Oceano Lagoon

OCEANO CAMPGROUND

P

ENTRANCE STATION

NATURE CENTER

PIER AVENUE

1

TO OCEAN AND HIKE 45

OCEANO LAGOON

Hike 45
Pismo Dunes

Hiking distance: 2 or more miles round trip
Hiking time: 1 hour
Elevation gain: 100 feet
Maps: U.S.G.S. Oceano
Pismo State Beach map

Summary of hike: The Pismo Dunes Recreation Area is an all-terrain vehicle playground. The hike begins in this area on the hard-packed oceanfront sand. The shoreline can be busy with cars, trucks and various motorized vehicles. A short distance ahead, the trail enters the undeveloped peaceful solitude of the most extensive coastal dunes in California. The hike meanders through the quiet and fragile natural preserve, crossing scrub-covered, wind-sculpted dunes.

Driving directions: From Highway 101 in Pismo Beach, take the Pismo Beach/Highway 1 South exit. Take Highway 1 through the town of Pismo Beach (Dolliver Street, which becomes Pacific Boulevard) for 3 miles to Pier Avenue. Turn right and drive 0.4 miles to the Pismo Beach State Park parking lot at the beachfront.

Hiking directions: Head south across the hard-packed sand between the ocean and the dunes. Hike 0.3 miles to Arroyo Grande Creek, passing beachfront homes along the way. After crossing the creek, curve left, entering the scrub-covered dunes at one of the many access trails. Meander south across the dunes, following the various interconnecting trails. Choose your own turnaround spot. On the return, continue north until reaching Arroyo Grande Creek. Follow the creek west, returning to the beach near the trailhead.

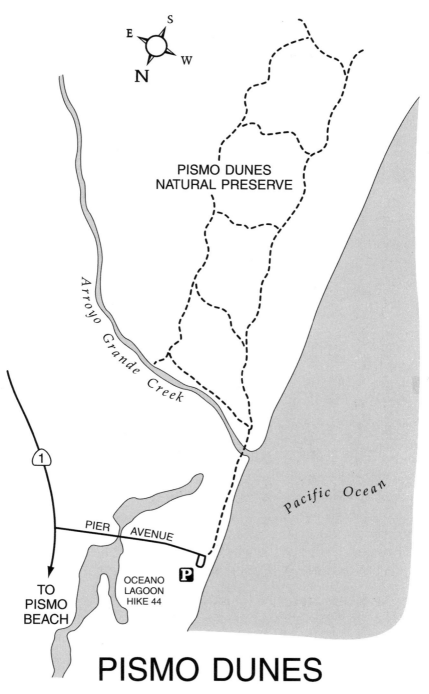

N
S
E
W

PISMO DUNES
NATURAL PRESERVE

SAN LUIS OBISPO COUNTY

Pacific Ocean

1

PIER AVENUE

TO
PISMO
BEACH

P

OCEANO
LAGOON
HIKE 44

PISMO DUNES

Hike 46
Black Lake
Free docent-led hike by
The Land Conservancy of San Luis Obispo County
Call (805) 544-9096 for scheduled hikes

Hiking distance: 2 miles round trip
Hiking time: 2 hours
Elevation gain: 100 feet
Maps: U.S.G.S. Oceano

Summary of hike: Black Lake is named for the color of the water, blackened by peat deposits beneath the lake. The lake sits in a natural depression nestled in the dunes and bordered by private property. It is formed from fresh water perched from the water table. The hike circles Black Lake through eucalyptus groves and coastal dune scrub. The views extend across the dunes to the Pacific Ocean.

Driving directions: From Highway 101 in Pismo Beach, take the Pismo Beach/Highway 1 South exit. Follow Highway 1 through the town of Pismo Beach (Dolliver Street, which becomes Pacific Boulevard) for 8.3 miles. Turn right on an unpaved road (0.5 miles north of Callender Road). Cautiously cross the railroad tracks, and continue 0.1 mile past the gate. Park on the left by the firewood racks.

From Highway 101 in Nipomo, take the Tefft Street exit, and head 0.6 miles west to Pomeroy Road. Turn right and drive 2.3 miles to Willow Road on the left. Turn left and go 2.5 miles, merging with Highway 1/Cabrillo Highway. Continue 2.4 miles to an unpaved road on the left, 0.5 miles north of Callender Road. Turn left and follow directions above.

Hiking directions: Begin the hike under a stately grove of eucalypti. Head south along the two-track road. Cross over a small hill through coastal dune scrub and sagebrush. From atop the hill are the first views of Black Lake. Descend to a junction, beginning the loop. Take the left fork, and cross the wetlands.

The wide path curves right and climbs a hill to a row of large eucalypti bordering a meadow. Continue along the meadow, through another eucalyptus grove, to the sand dunes at the west end of the lake. Descend the ridge and loop around the lake to a T-junction. Bear to the right and complete the loop. Return to the left.

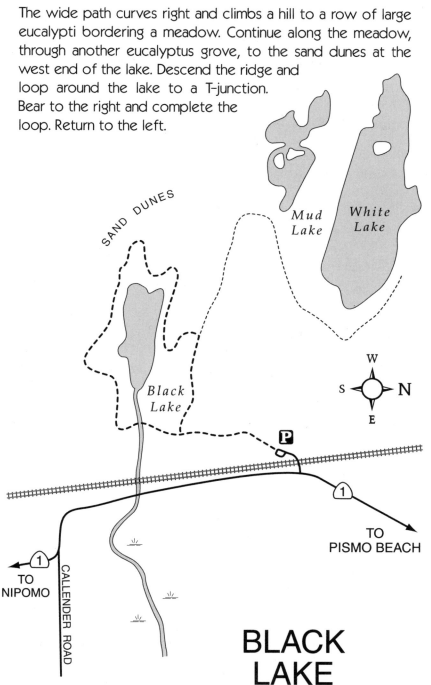

Mud Lake

White Lake

W

S — N

E

SAND DUNES

Black Lake

P

1

TO PISMO BEACH

TO NIPOMO

1

CALLENDER ROAD

BLACK LAKE

Hike 47
Oso Flaco Lake Trail

Hiking distance: 2.2 miles round trip
Hiking time: 1 hour
Elevation gain: Level
Maps: U.S.G.S. Oceano
Oso Flaco Lake Natural Area map

Summary of hike: Oso Flaco Lake is located at the south end of the Pismo Dunes Natural Preserve. The trail crosses a footbridge over the 75-acre lake and wetlands preserve. The freshwater lake is surrounded by cattails, sedges, wax myrtle and willows. It is a great place for watching birds and wildlife. A wooden boardwalk leads through the Nipomo Dunes and wetlands area, minimizing damage to the fragile plant life. The boardwalk ends at the ocean.

Driving directions: From Highway 101 in Nipomo, take the Tefft Street exit, and head 0.8 miles west to Orchard Road. Turn left and drive 0.7 miles to Division Street. Turn right and continue 3.2 miles to Oso Flaco Lake Road. Bear right and go 5.3 miles to the Oso Flaco Lake parking lot at the end of the road. A parking fee is required.

Hiking directions: Head west on the paved road past the trailhead gate and through the shady cottonwood forest to the shores of Oso Flaco Lake. Bear left on the long footbridge spanning the lake. From the west end of the lake, continue on a wooden boardwalk that ambles across the fragile coastal dunes. Most of the trail follows the boardwalk except for a short, well-marked sandy stretch. The boardwalk ends at the ocean on a long and wide stretch of sandy beach at 1.1 miles. To the south is the Mobil Coastal Preserve and Coreopsis Hill, a large dune. To the north is the Pismo Dunes (Hike 45) and the Santa Maria River. Explore at your own pace up and down the coastline. Return on the boardwalk.

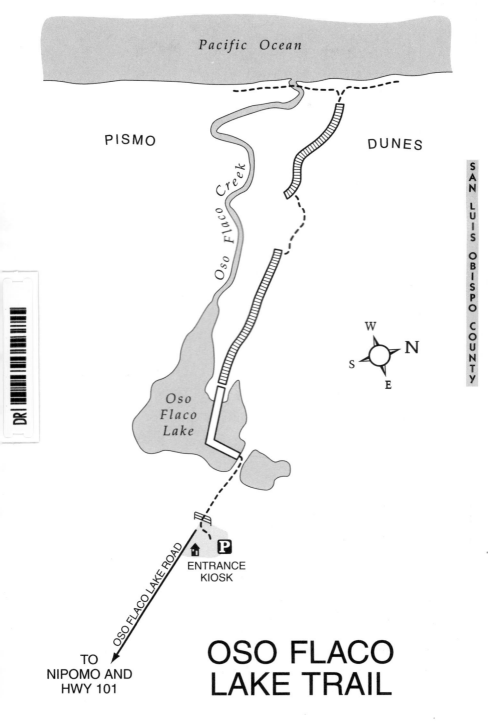

Pacific Ocean

PISMO

DUNES

Oso Flaco Creek

SAN LUIS OBISPO COUNTY

Oso
Flaco
Lake

W
S ○ N
E

OSO FLACO LAKE ROAD

ENTRANCE
KIOSK

TO
NIPOMO AND
HWY 101

OSO FLACO
LAKE TRAIL

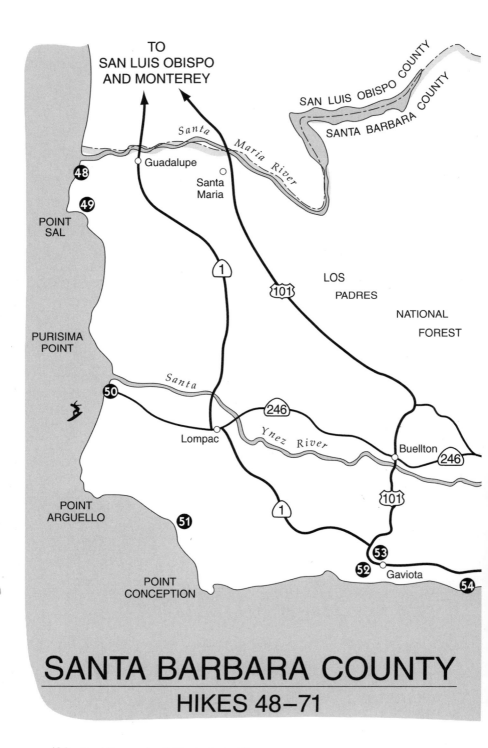

SANTA BARBARA COUNTY
HIKES 48–71

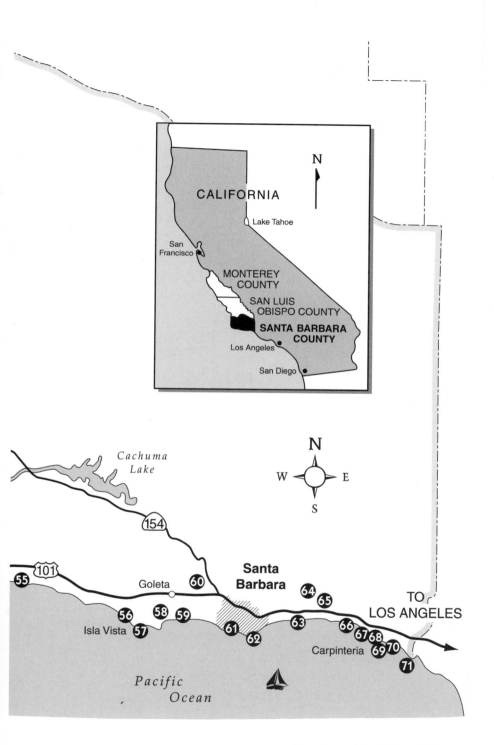

Hike 48
Guadalupe-Nipomo Dunes Preserve
to Mussel Rock

Hiking distance: 6 miles round trip
Hiking time: 3 hours
Elevation gain: Level
Maps: U.S.G.S. Point Sal

Summary of hike: The Guadalupe-Nipomo Dunes Preserve sits among a range of towering, rolling sand mountains. This hike follows the isolated shoreline along the sandy beach, parallel to the highest sand dunes on the west coast. The north end of the preserve is bordered by the Santa Maria River on the county line. At the mouth of the river is a wetland area, providing a habitat for migrating shorebirds and native waterfowl. The south end of the dune complex is bordered by Mussel Rock, a 450-foot promontory jutting out into the sea.

Driving directions: From Highway 101 in Santa Maria, take the Main Street/Highway 166 exit, and head west towards Guadalupe. Drive 11.7 miles, passing Guadalupe, to the Guadalupe-Nipomo Dunes Preserve entrance. Continue 2 miles to the parking area on the oceanfront.

Hiking directions: Walk to the shoreline. First head north a half mile to the mouth of the Santa Maria River. The river widens out, forming a lagoon at the base of scrub-covered dunes. At low tide, a sandbar separates the river estuary from the ocean, allowing easy access from the north along the Nipomo Dunes. Return to the south, meandering along the beach. Various side paths lead inland and up into the dunes. Follow the coastline to the cliffs of Mussel Rock at 3 miles. The enormous, jagged formation extends out into the ocean. For great coastal views to Point Sal, head a short distance up Mussel Rock to a sandy path that contours around to the south side of the formation. Return back along the beach to the parking area.

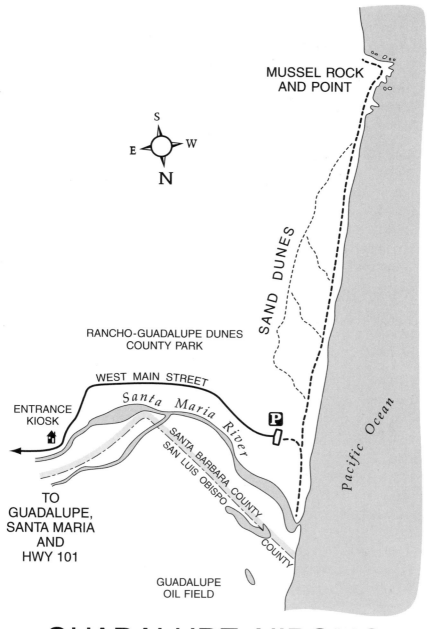

MUSSEL ROCK
AND POINT

S
E ✧ W
N

SAND DUNES

RANCHO-GUADALUPE DUNES
COUNTY PARK

WEST MAIN STREET

Santa Maria River

Pacific Ocean

ENTRANCE
KIOSK

🏠

P

SANTA BARBARA COUNTY
SAN LUIS OBISPO COUNTY

TO
GUADALUPE,
SANTA MARIA
AND
HWY 101

GUADALUPE
OIL FIELD

S A N T A   B A R B A R A   C O U N T Y

GUADALUPE-NIPOMO
DUNES PRESERVE

Hike 49
Point Sal Overlook

Hiking distance: 4 miles round trip
Hiking time: 2 hours
Elevation gain: 600 feet
Maps: U.S.G.S. Point Sal and Guadalupe

Summary of hike: This hike follows an old road through the rolling Casmalia Hills to several panoramic overlooks. The road, which crosses into Vandenberg Air Force Base, is open only to foot traffic due to unstable soil and washouts. The spectacular views include Point Sal Ridge to Point Sal, the secluded Point Sal Beach at the base of the bluffs, Lion Rock, Point Arguello to the south, and north to Point Buchon at Montaña de Oro State Park.

Driving directions: From Highway 101 in Santa Maria, take the Betteravia exit, and head 7.7 miles west to Brown Road. Turn left and continue 5.1 miles to the signed junction with the Point Sal Road on the right. Turn right and park by the road gate.

Hiking directions: Walk past the locked gate, and follow the road uphill along the west edge of Corralitos Canyon. At 0.3 miles, the paved road turns to dirt, reaching a horseshoe bend at a half mile. Leave Corralitos Canyon and head south, reaching the first ocean overlook at one mile. Continue gently uphill, crossing Point Sal Ridge to a cattle guard at a fenceline. The road enters Vandenberg Air Force Base and becomes paved again. A short distance ahead is an abandoned cinder block building on the left with a wide stairway up to the concrete roof. From this overlook are commanding views up and down the scalloped coastline. Return to the road, and descend a few hundred yards to another overlook. The view extends along Point Sal Ridge to Point Sal. This is our turnaround spot.

To hike further, the road continues another 3 miles, descending 1,200 feet to the ocean. At the road fork, bear right. Near the shore, scramble down to the remote beach at Point Sal Beach State Park.

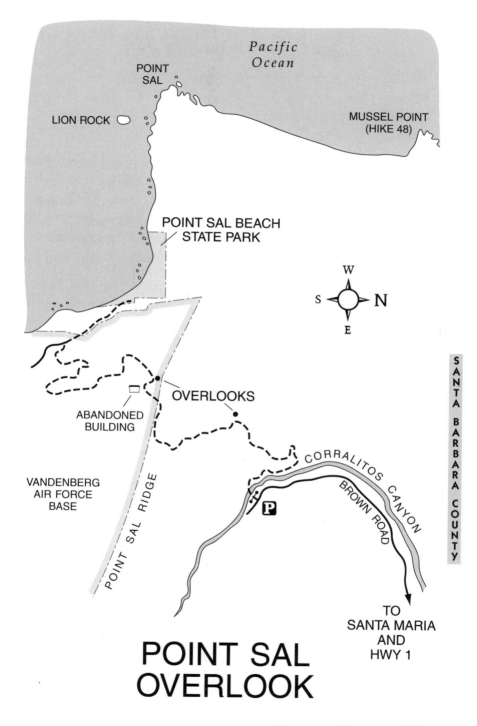

POINT SAL
OVERLOOK

Hike 50
Ocean Beach County Park

Hiking distance: 7 miles round trip
Hiking time: 3 hours
Elevation gain: Level
Maps: U.S.G.S. Surf and Point Arguello

Summary of hike: Ocean Beach is a 36-acre park between Purisima Point and Point Arguello. The park borders the Santa Ynez River by a 400-acre lagoon and marsh at the mouth of the river. It is a resting and foraging habitat for migrating birds and waterfowl. Vandenberg Air Force Base, which surrounds the park, allows beach access for 1.5 miles north and 3.5 miles south.

Driving directions: From Santa Barbara, drive 35 miles northbound on Highway 101 to the Highway 1/Lompoc exit. Turn left and drive 17.7 miles to the Highway 246/Ocean Avenue junction in Lompoc. Turn left and continue 9.5 miles to Ocean Park Road. Turn right and go one mile to the parking lot at the end of the road by the Santa Ynez River.

From Highway 101 in Buellton, take the Highway 246 exit. Drive 25.7 miles west, passing through Lompoc, to Ocean Park Road. (Highway 246 becomes Ocean Avenue in Lompoc.) Turn right and go one mile to the parking lot at the end of the road.

Hiking directions: To the north, a path borders the lagoon with interpretive nature panels. After enjoying the estuary, take the quarter-mile paved path following the south bank of the Santa Ynez River. Cross under the railroad trestle to the wide sandy beach. (Or take the footpath over the hill and cross the tracks.) Walk past the dunes to the shoreline at the mouth of the river. A sandbar separates the ocean from the river, allowing access up the coast. This hike heads south along the coastline. The wide beach narrows to a strip at one mile. Vandenberg Air Force Base sits atop the cliffs. At just over 3 miles the beach ends as the cliffs meet the reef. Point Pedernales can be seen ahead, extending out to sea. Return the way you came.

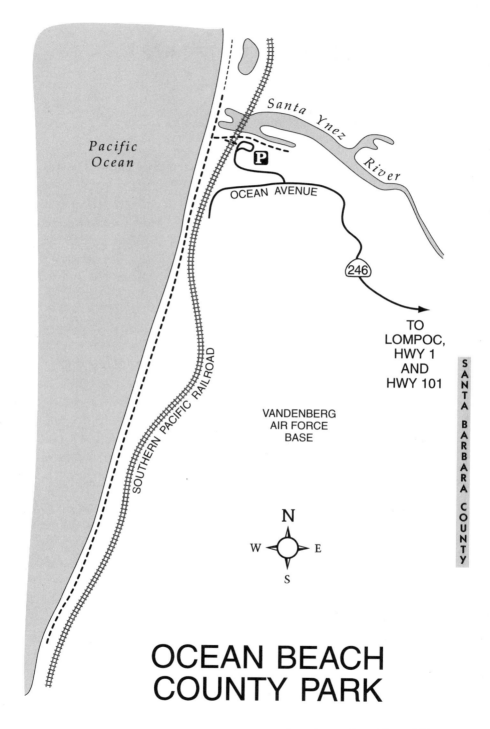

**OCEAN BEACH
COUNTY PARK**

Hike 51
Jalama Beach County Park

Hiking distance: 2 miles round trip
Hiking time: 1 hour
Elevation gain: Level
Maps: U.S.G.S. Lompoc Hills and Tranquillon Mountain

Summary of hike: Jalama Beach County Park is a picturesque 28-acre park at the mouth of Jalama Creek between Point Arguello and Point Conception. The park includes a year-round campground with a half mile of shoreline, a small wetland habitat, a picnic area and general store. This isolated stretch of coastline is backed by cliffs and lush, rolling hills. For centuries it was a Chumash Indian settlement. It is now bordered by Vandenberg Air Force Base.

Driving directions: From Santa Barbara, drive 35 miles northbound on Highway 101 to the Highway 1/Lompoc exit. Turn left and drive 13.5 miles to Jalama Road. Turn left and continue 14 miles to the oceanfront campground and parking lot. A parking fee is required.

From Highway 101 in Buellton, take the Highway 246 exit. Drive 16.2 miles west to Highway 1 in Lompoc. Turn left and continue 4.2 miles to Jalama Road. Turn right and continue 14 miles to the campground and parking lot.

Hiking directions: Follow the shoreline north for a short distance to the park boundary at Jalama Creek. The bluffs above the creek are fenced, but you may beachcomb northwest for a mile beyond the creek to the Vandenberg Air Force Base boundary. Heading south, the sandy beach narrows and ends along the seawall cliffs. At low tide, the shoreline can be followed along the rock formations.

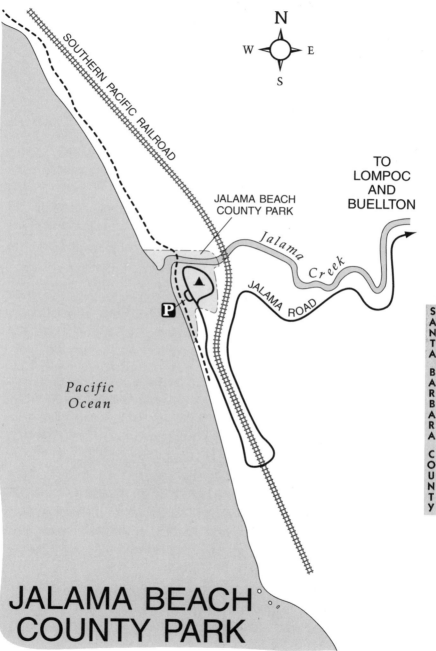

N

W ←◇→ E

S

SOUTHERN PACIFIC RAILROAD

JALAMA BEACH
COUNTY PARK

TO
LOMPOC
AND
BUELLTON

Jalama *Creek*

JALAMA ROAD

P

Pacific
Ocean

JALAMA BEACH
COUNTY PARK

SANTA BARBARA COUNTY

Hike 52
Beach to Backcountry Trail
Gaviota State Park

Hiking distance: 3 miles round trip
Hiking time: 1.5 hours
Elevation gain: 750 feet
Maps: U.S.G.S. Gaviota
       Gaviota State Park map

Summary of hike: In the mountainous backcountry of the 2,775-acre Gaviota State Park, a network of trails lead to scenic overlooks, sandstone outcroppings with intriguing caves and oak-studded rolling hills. This hike follows the Beach To Backcountry Trail across the rolling terrain to a vista point high above Gaviota Pass. There are great views of Gaviota Peak, the Pacific Ocean and the Channel Islands.

Driving directions: From Santa Barbara, drive 33 miles northbound on Highway 101 to the Gaviota State Beach turnoff on the left. Turn left and drive 0.4 miles, bearing right near the entrance kiosk. Drive to the trailhead parking area on the right.

Hiking directions: Head north past the locked gate on the paved road. The half-mile road leads through dense scrub brush. A hundred yards before the road ends is a signed multi-purpose trail on the left—the Beach to Backcountry Trail. Take this footpath up the south-facing hillside of the canyon. On the way up, views open to the Pacific Ocean and Gaviota Peak (Hike 53). The trail steadily zigzags up to a ridge. At one mile the trail levels out near large, sculpted sandstone outcroppings and caves. Begin a second ascent to the largest formation, and curve around to the backside of the outcropping. Cross a ravine and continue uphill to the top and a junction with the Overlook Fire Road. The left fork heads north into the mountainous interior of Gaviota State Park. Take the right fork a half mile to a panoramic overlook at the radio tower and building. After enjoying the views, return by retracing your steps.

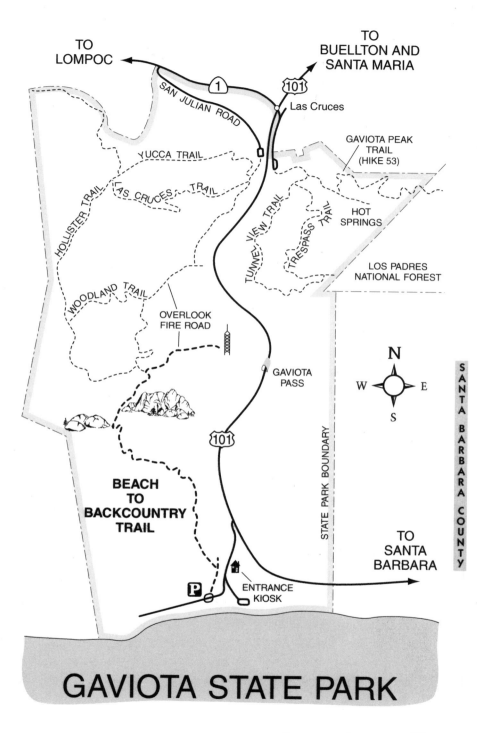

GAVIOTA STATE PARK

Hike 53
Gaviota Peak

Hiking distance: 6 miles round trip
Hiking time: 3 hours
Elevation gain: 1,900 feet
Maps: U.S.G.S. Solvang and Gaviota
Gaviota State Park map

Summary of hike: The trail to Gaviota Peak begins in Gaviota State Park and ends in the Los Padres National Forest. The trail passes Gaviota Hot Springs, a series of lukewarm, primitive sulphur spring pools that are popular for soaking. The hike to the peak is a substantial workout, but the views of the Santa Ynez Mountains, Lompoc Valley, the Pacific Ocean and the Channel Islands are spectacular.

Driving directions: From Santa Barbara, drive 35 miles northbound on Highway 101 to the Highway 1 and Lompoc/Vandenberg AFB exit. Turn sharply to the right onto the frontage road, and continue 0.3 miles to the Gaviota State Park parking lot at the road's end.

Hiking directions: Hike east past the trailhead on the wide, unpaved road under the shade of oak and sycamore trees. Stay on the main trail past a junction with the Trespass Trail. Cross a stream to a junction at 0.4 miles. The right fork is a short side trip to Gaviota Hot Springs. After enjoying the springs, return to the junction and continue on the left fork, following the old road as it curves around the grassy hillside. From here, there are views of the rolling hills and ranches of the Lompoc Valley. Long, gradual switchbacks lead up to the national forest boundary at 1.5 miles. At two miles, the trail reaches a saddle with more great views. The grade of the trail is never steep, but it rarely levels out. Near the top, pass a metal gate to a junction. Take the right fork for the final ascent to the peak and the spectacular views. Return along the same trail.

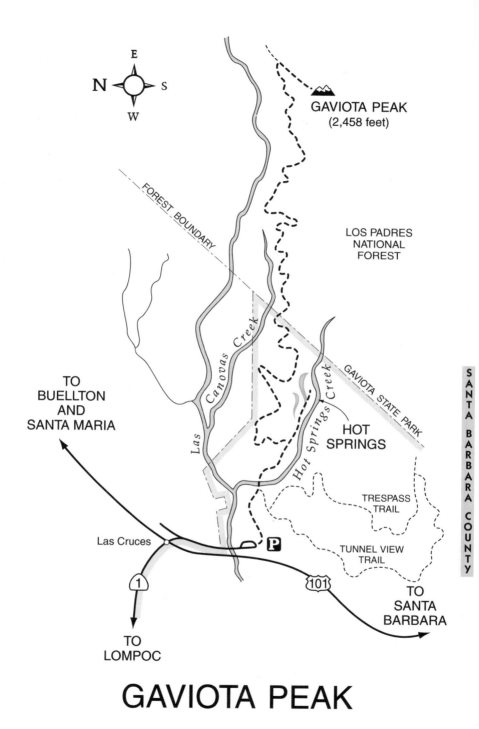

GAVIOTA PEAK
(2,458 feet)

LOS PADRES
NATIONAL
FOREST

FOREST BOUNDARY

Las Canovas Creek

Hot Springs Creek

GAVIOTA STATE PARK

TO
BUELLTON
AND
SANTA MARIA

HOT
SPRINGS

TRESPASS
TRAIL

Las Cruces

TUNNEL VIEW
TRAIL

P

1

101

TO
SANTA
BARBARA

TO
LOMPOC

S A N T A   B A R B A R A   C O U N T Y

GAVIOTA PEAK

Hike 54
Aniso Trail
El Capitan State Beach to Refugio State Beach

Hiking distance: 5 miles round trip
Hiking time: 2.5 hours
Elevation gain: Near level
Maps: U.S.G.S. Tajiguas

Summary of hike: The Aniso Trail (Chumash for seagull) is a paved hiking and biking trail along the sea cliffs and marine terraces connecting El Capitan State Beach to Refugio State Beach. The trail, an ancient Chumash trade route, follows the bluffs past weathered rock formations and secluded coves, offering constant views of the coastline. El Capitan State Beach sits at the mouth of El Capitan Creek in a extensive riparian woodland of coastal oaks and sycamores. Refugio State Beach, at the mouth of Refugio Canyon, has a palm-lined sandy beach cove and rocky shoreline with tidepools. Refugio Creek meanders through the park.

Driving directions: From Santa Barbara, drive 20 miles northbound on Highway 101 to the El Capitan State Beach exit. It is located 0.8 miles past the El Capitan Ranch Road exit. Turn left (south) and drive 0.3 miles to the state park entrance. Park in the day-use lot straight ahead.

Hiking directions: The paved trail begins on the north (right) side of the general store. Head west, skirting around the edge of the campground, and follow the contours of the cliffs past a lifeguard station. Two side paths descend to the beach and marine terraces. Descend from the bluffs to the beach at the south end of Corral Canyon. A side path curves left to the ocean. Continue straight ahead, returning to the bluffs past weathered rock formations. At 2.5 miles, the trail enters Refugio State Park near the palm-lined bay. Refugio Creek forms a tropical-looking freshwater lagoon near the ocean. After exploring the park, return the way you came.

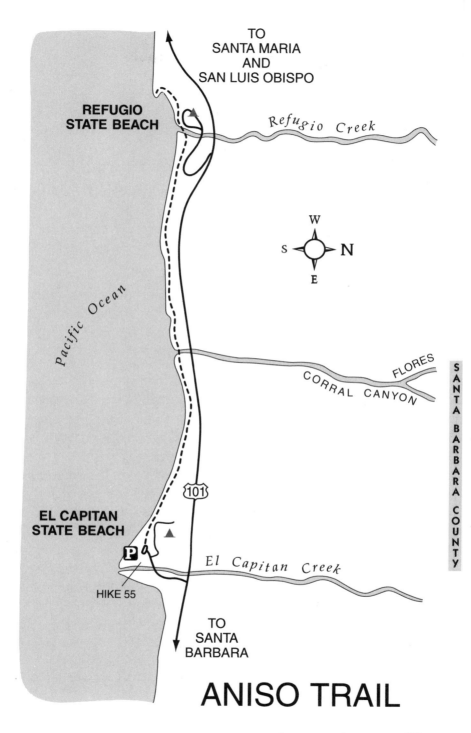

TO
SANTA MARIA
AND
SAN LUIS OBISPO

REFUGIO
STATE BEACH

Refugio Creek

W
S — N
E

Pacific Ocean

FLORES

CORRAL CANYON

101

EL CAPITAN
STATE BEACH

▲

P

El Capitan Creek

HIKE 55

TO
SANTA
BARBARA

ANISO TRAIL

Hike 55
El Capitan State Beach

Hiking distance: 1.5 miles round trip
Hiking time: 1 hour
Elevation gain: Level
Maps: U.S.G.S. Tajiguas
          El Capitan and Refugio State Beach—Park Service Map

Summary of hike: Located west of Santa Barbara, El Capitan State Beach has a beautiful sandy beach with rocky tidepools. El Capitan Creek flows through a forested canyon to the tidepools. Nature trails weave through stands of sycamore and oak trees alongside the creek.

Driving directions: From Santa Barbara, drive 20 miles northbound on Highway 101 to the El Capitan State Beach exit. It is located 0.8 miles past the El Capitan Ranch Road exit. Turn left (south) and drive 0.3 miles to the state park entrance. Park in the day-use lot straight ahead.

Hiking directions: For a short walk, take the paved path down the hillside from the general store to the oceanfront. The quarter-mile paved trail follows the shoreline a short distance to the east before looping back to the parking lot.

For a longer hike, continue along the shore on the unpaved path past a grassy picnic area to El Capitan Creek. Near the mouth of the creek are the tidepools. Take the "Nature Trail" footpath, heading inland through the woodlands while following El Capitan Creek upstream. You will pass several intersecting trails that loop back to the park entrance station and parking lot. Near the entrance station, pick up the trail on the west side of the road. The trail parallels the western edge of El Capitan Creek through the forested canyon. The trail ends at a railroad bridge where the trail meets the road. Return by reversing your route or by exploring one of the intersecting nature trails.

To continue hiking along the shore to Refugio State Beach, take the Aniso Trail—Hike 54.

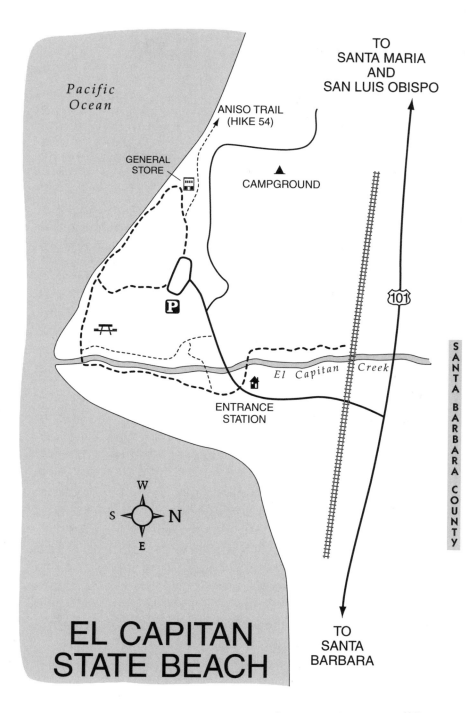

Pacific
Ocean

ANISO TRAIL
(HIKE 54)

GENERAL
STORE

CAMPGROUND

TO
SANTA MARIA
AND
SAN LUIS OBISPO

P

El Capitan Creek

ENTRANCE
STATION

101

SANTA BARBARA COUNTY

W
S — N
E

EL CAPITAN
STATE BEACH

TO
SANTA
BARBARA

Hike 56
Ellwood Bluffs Trail
Santa Barbara Shores

Hiking distance: 3.5 miles round trip
Hiking time: 1.5 hours
Elevation gain: Level
Maps: U.S.G.S. Dos Pueblos Canyon
Santa Barbara County Recreational Map Series #8

Summary of hike: Santa Barbara Shores County Park has a network of interconnecting trails across flat grasslands overlooking the Pacific Ocean. The Ellwood Bluffs Trail parallels 80-foot high cliffs along the ocean's edge. The eucalyptus groves are home to monarch butterflies during the winter months.

Driving directions: From Santa Barbara, drive northbound on Highway 101 to the Glen Annie Road/Storke Road exit in Goleta. Turn left on Storke Road, and drive 0.3 miles to Hollister Avenue, the first intersection. Turn right and continue 1.7 miles to the Santa Barbara County Park parking lot on the left, just past Ellwood School.

Hiking directions: At the trailhead is a junction. Take the right fork along the western edge of the parkland. The trail parallels a row of mature eucalyptus trees separating the Santa Barbara Shores County Park from the Sandpiper Golf Course. Continue south to the bluffs overlooking the ocean. Follow the trail to the left along the cliff's edge. Several trails cut across the open space to the left, returning to the trailhead for a shorter hike. At 0.5 miles is a junction with a beach access trail heading down to the mile-long beach. Further along the bluffs, take the trail inland, heading north along a row of eucalyptus trees. As you approach the eucalyptus groves, return along the prominent footpath to the left. The trail returns to the trailhead on the edge of the open meadows next to the groves.

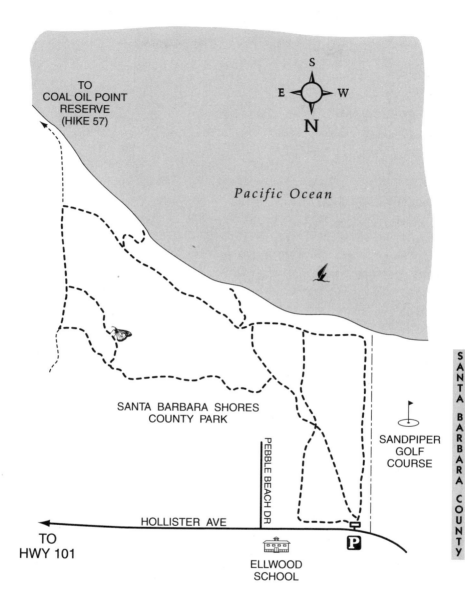

ELLWOOD BLUFFS TRAIL
SANTA BARBARA SHORES

Hike 57
Coal Oil Point Reserve

Hiking distance: 3 miles round trip
Hiking time: 1.5 hours
Elevation gain: Near level
Maps: U.S.G.S. Goleta and Dos Pueblos Canyon
        The Thomas Guide—Santa Barbara and Vicinity

Summary of hike: Coal Oil Point Reserve has several coastal wildlife habitats set aside for research, education and preservation. The 117-acre ecological study enclave, managed by UCSB, has coastal dunes, eucalyptus groves, grasslands, a salt marsh and a 45-acre lagoon. The trail parallels the bluffs from the western edge of Isla Vista to the reserve. Devereaux Lagoon, with a mixture of fresh water and salt water, provides several coastal lagoon habitats. The slough is a bird-watcher's paradise with a wide variety of native and migratory species.

Driving directions: From Santa Barbara, drive northbound on Highway 101 to the Glen Annie Road/Storke Road exit in Goleta. Turn left on Storke Road, and drive 1.3 miles to El Colegio Road. Turn left and drive 0.2 miles to Camino Corto. Turn right and continue 0.5 miles to Del Playa Drive. Turn right and park in the parking area at the end of the block.

Hiking directions: Take the well-defined path to the ocean bluffs and a T-junction. To the left, a stairway descends to the beach, and the blufftop path continues 0.2 miles to Del Playa Park and Isla Vista County Beach. Take the right fork, parallel to the edge of the cliffs, passing through a eucalyptus grove. Several surfing paths lead down the cliffs to the sandy beach and rocky tidepools. The main trail leads to the Coal Oil Point Reserve. Pass through the habitat gate to Sands Beach. Several paths meander across the dunes to Devereaux Lagoon. A path circles the lagoon, returning on the paved roadway along the east side of the slough. You may also follow the beach for another mile northwest, reaching the Ellwood Bluffs (Hike 56).

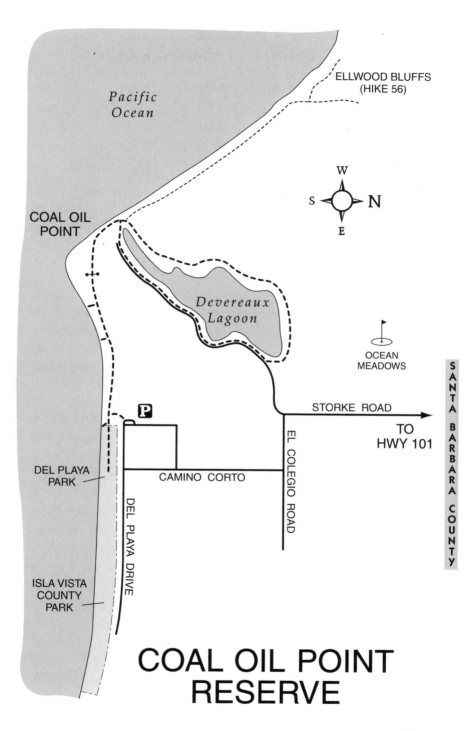

Pacific Ocean

ELLWOOD BLUFFS
(HIKE 56)

COAL OIL
POINT

W

S ☼ N

E

Devereaux Lagoon

OCEAN
MEADOWS

STORKE ROAD

TO
HWY 101

P

EL COLEGIO ROAD

DEL PLAYA
PARK

CAMINO CORTO

DEL PLAYA DRIVE

ISLA VISTA
COUNTY
PARK

COAL OIL POINT
RESERVE

Hike 58
Goleta Beach and the UCSB Lagoon

Hiking distance: 4 miles round trip
Hiking time: 2 hours
Elevation gain: 50 feet
Maps: U.S.G.S. Goleta
   The Thomas Guide—Santa Barbara & Vicinity

Summary of hike: This trail begins at Goleta Beach County Park and follows the coastal cliffs into the University of California—Santa Barbara. The trail circles the UCSB Lagoon to Goleta Point. The ocean surrounds the point on three sides, where there are tidepools and a beautiful coastline.

Driving directions: From Highway 101 in Goleta, exit onto Ward Memorial Boulevard/Highway 217. Continue 2 miles to the Sandspit Road exit, and turn left at the stop sign, heading towards Goleta Beach Park. Drive 0.3 miles to the beach parking lot turnoff. Turn right and cross the lagoon into the parking lot.

Hiking directions: Hike west along the park lawn to the bluffs overlooking the ocean. Continue past the natural bridge. The path parallels the cliff edge into the university. At the marine laboratory, take the right fork, crossing the road to the UCSB Lagoon. The lagoon sits on Goleta Point. Take the path to the right around the northeast side of the lagoon. At the north end, the trail joins a walking path in the university. At the west end of the lagoon, the trail heads south on the return portion of the loop. Once back at the ocean, climb up the bluff to the left. Continue around the lagoon, and descend the steps between the lagoon and the ocean. Complete the loop back at the marine laboratory and bluffs. Head east, back to Goleta Beach Park.

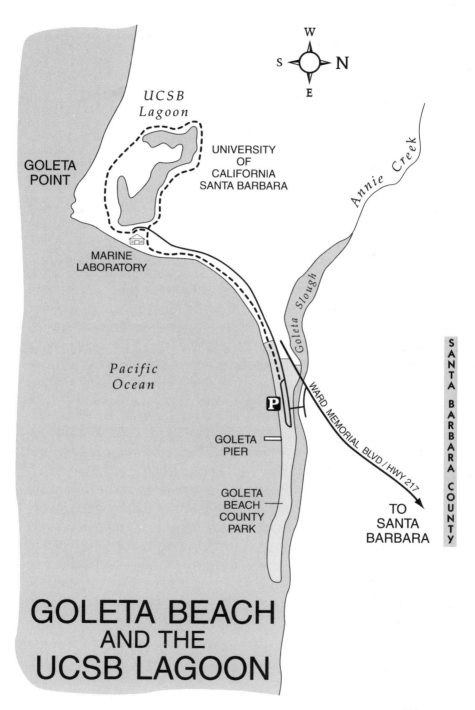

GOLETA BEACH
AND THE
UCSB LAGOON

Hike 59
More Mesa

Hiking distance: 2.6 miles round trip
Hiking time: 1.5 hours
Elevation gain: Near level
Maps: U.S.G.S. Goleta
   The Thomas Guide—Santa Barbara and Vicinity

Summary of hike: More Mesa is an undeveloped 300-acre oceanfront expanse in Goleta. The flat blufftop mesa is marbled with hiking trails. The main trail follows the edge of the bluffs 200 feet above the ocean. The panoramic views extend from the Santa Ynez Mountains to the Channel Islands. The secluded, mile-long beach at the base of the mesa is clothing optional.

Driving directions: From Santa Barbara, drive northbound on Highway 101, and exit on Turnpike Road in Goleta. Turn left and drive 0.4 miles to Hollister Avenue. Turn left and go 0.3 miles to the first signal at Puente Drive. Turn right and continue 0.7 miles to Mockingbird Lane. Along the way Puente Drive becomes Vieja Drive. Parking is not allowed on Mockingbird Lane, so park on Vieja Drive by Mockingbird Lane.

Hiking directions: Walk up Mockingbird Lane to the hiking path at the end of the street. Pass the metal trailhead gate, and cross the wide, flat marine terrace towards the ocean. At 0.6 miles, the path reaches a grove of mature eucalyptus trees lining the edge of the cliffs 200 feet above the ocean. A steep, narrow path descends down the cliffs to the secluded sandy beach. The left fork leads a short distance to a fenced residential area. Take the right fork, following the edge of the bluffs to the west. At 1.3 miles, the trail crosses a fenceline and ends by oceanfront homes. Various interconnecting trails crisscross the open space. Return along the same route for the best views.

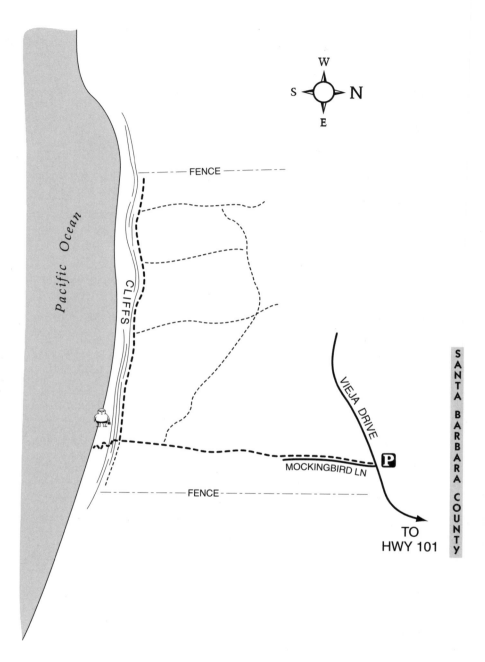

MORE MESA

Hike 60
San Antonio Creek Trail

Hiking distance: 3.4 miles round trip
Hiking time: 1.5 hours
Elevation gain: 200 feet
Maps: U.S.G.S. Goleta
   Santa Barbara Front Country Recreational Map

Summary of hike: The San Antonio Creek Trail begins at the far end of Tuckers Grove County Park in Goleta. The level trail follows San Antonio Canyon along the watercourse of the creek through grassy meadows and a shady woodland of bay laurel, oak and sycamore trees.

Driving directions: From Santa Barbara, drive northbound on Highway 101, and exit on Turnpike Road in Goleta. Drive 0.6 miles north to Cathedral Oaks Road. Drive straight through the intersection, entering Tuckers Grove Park. Bear to the right through the parking lot, and drive 0.3 miles to the last parking area.

Hiking directions: From the parking lot, hike up the road and past the upper picnic ground, Kiwanis Meadow. Cross through the opening in the log fence to the left, heading towards the creek. Take the trail upstream along the east side of San Antonio Creek. Numerous spur trails lead down to the creek. At one mile, rock hop across the creek, and continue to a second crossing located between steep canyon walls. After crossing, the trail ascends a hill to a bench near a concrete flood-control dam. Head left across the top of the dam. The trail proceeds to the right, upstream, and recrosses San Antonio Creek. The forested canyon trail passes alongside a chainlink fence on the east side of the stream. The trail ends at 1.7 miles under a bridge where the trail intersects with Highway 154. Return along the same trail.

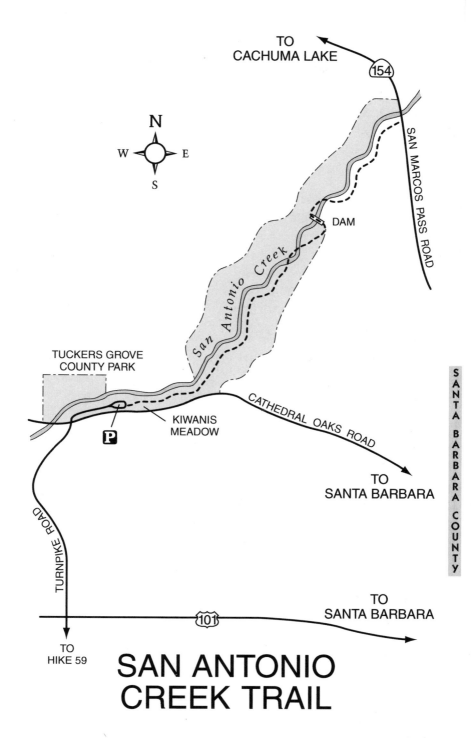

SAN ANTONIO
CREEK TRAIL

TO CACHUMA LAKE

154

SAN MARCOS PASS ROAD

DAM

San Antonio Creek

TUCKERS GROVE
COUNTY PARK

P

KIWANIS
MEADOW

CATHEDRAL OAKS ROAD

**TO
SANTA BARBARA**

TURNPIKE ROAD

101

**TO
SANTA BARBARA**

TO
HIKE 59

Hike 61
Santa Barbara Coastal Bluffs

Hiking distance: 1.5 miles round trip
Hiking time: 1 hour
Elevation gain: 200 feet
Maps: U.S.G.S. Santa Barbara
The Thomas Guide—Santa Barbara & Vicinity

Summary of hike: The Santa Barbara Coastal Bluffs, also known as The Douglas Family Preserve, is a 70-acre grassy mesa with over 2,200 feet of rare, undeveloped ocean frontage. The preserve is covered with mature oaks, eucalyptus, and cypress trees. The trail loops around the mesa along the edge of the cliffs. Below the cliffs is the picturesque Arroyo Burro Beach, locally known as Hendry's Beach. There are picnic areas and a paved biking and walking path.

Driving directions: From Highway 101 in Santa Barbara, exit on Las Positas Road. Head 1.8 miles south (towards the ocean) to Cliff Drive and turn right. Continue 0.2 miles to the Arroyo Burro Beach parking lot on the left and park.

Hiking directions: From the parking lot, walk east on Cliff Drive to Las Positas Road. From here, a trail heads south past a chained gate into the forest. The trail curves left through the shady canopy up the hill. At the top, the trail levels out. Continue south along the eastern edge of the open space. Along the way several paths intersect from the right and several access trails come in from the left. At the bluffs overlooking the ocean, head west along the cliffs. At the west end of the cliffs is an overlook of Arroyo Burro Beach. The trail curves to the right and loops back to a junction at the top of the hill. Take a left, retracing your steps down the hill and back to the parking lot.

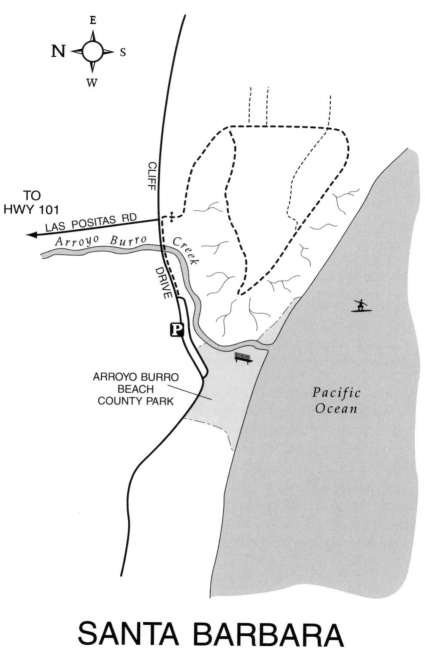

SANTA BARBARA
COASTAL BLUFFS

Hike 62
Shoreline Park

Hiking distance: 1—2 miles round trip
Hiking time: 30 minutes—1 hour
Elevation gain: Level
Maps: U.S.G.S. Santa Barbara
　　　　The Thomas Guide—Santa Barbara and Vicinity

Summary of hike: Shoreline Park is a 15-acre park along La Mesa Bluff with panoramic vistas of Leadbetter Beach, the Santa Barbara Harbor and the Channel Islands. The narrow, grassy park hugs the ocean bluffs on the west side of Santa Barbara Point. This paved path is an easy stroll along the marine terrace. A stairway leads down to the shore for a sandy beach stroll at the base of the cliffs.

Driving directions: From Stearns Wharf at the south end of State Street in Santa Barbara, drive 1.4 miles west on Cabrillo Boulevard (which becomes Shoreline Drive) to the first Shoreline Park parking lot on the left.

Hiking directions: The paved path heads west along the oceanfront bluffs between the cliff's edge and Shoreline Drive. At 0.3 miles, a stairway leads down to the sandy beach and shoreline. Along the way are benches and information stations about the Chumash Indians, the Channel Islands, grey whales and dolphins. A half mile ahead, at the west end of the park, is a picnic area and additional parking lot. Return along the same path. To continue hiking along the shoreline, return to the stairway and descend to the beach. Stroll along the sand beneath the cliffs.

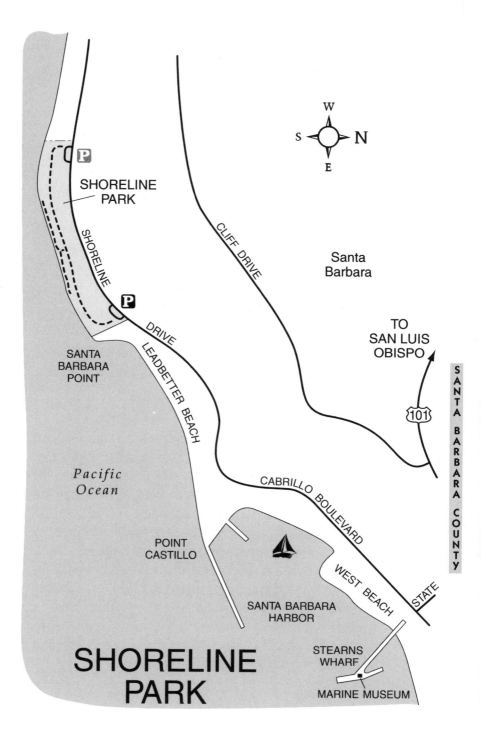

Hike 63
Hammonds Meadow Trail

Hiking distance: 2 miles round trip
Hiking time: 1 hour
Elevation gain: Level
Maps: U.S.G.S. Santa Barbara
      The Thomas Guide—Santa Barbara and Vicinity

Summary of hike: The Hammonds Meadow Trail strolls through a forest of palm and eucalyptus trees with tall, flowering bougainvillea bushes. The pastoral path connects three beaches between the Miramar and Biltmore Hotels. The walking path passes beautiful homes, crossing Montecito Creek to the beachfront.

Driving directions: From Santa Barbara, drive southbound on Highway 101 to Montecito, and exit on San Ysidro Road south. Turn right on Eucalyptus Lane, and drive south 0.1 mile to a small parking lot at the end of the road, just past Bonnymede Drive. If the lot is full, an additional parking area is on Humphrey Road, the first street north.

Hiking directions: The signed trail begins to the west. (A short detour straight ahead to the south leads down a few steps to a coastal access at Miramar Beach.) Take the Hammonds Meadow Trail through a beautiful forested lane surrounded by every color of flowering bougainvilleas. At 0.2 miles, a bridge crosses Montecito Creek. Along both sides of the creek are coastal access paths. Cross the bridge and parallel the west side of the creek to Hammonds Beach. Follow the shoreline to the west for a quarter mile, reaching the Biltmore Hotel at the east end of Butterfly Beach. Follow the coastline west on Butterfly Beach below the bluff terrace. Several staircases lead up to Channel Drive. This is our turnaround spot. After beachcombing, return along the same path.

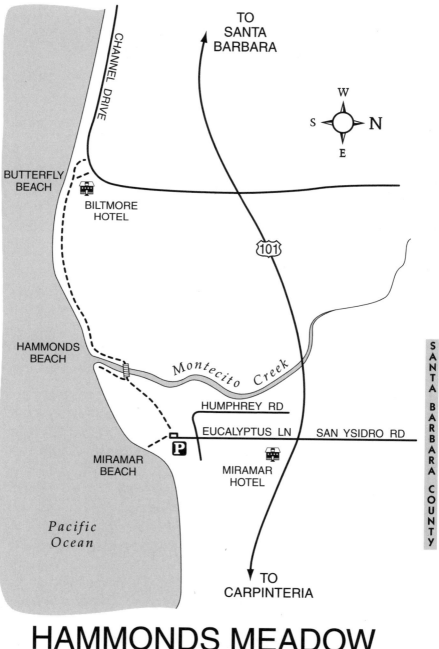

HAMMONDS MEADOW TRAIL

Hike 64
San Ysidro Canyon

Hiking distance: 3.7 miles round trip
Hiking time: 2 hours
Elevation gain: 1,200 feet
Maps: U.S.G.S. Carpinteria and Santa Barbara
      Santa Barbara Front Country Recreational Map

Summary of hike: The San Ysidro Trail heads up the picturesque San Ysidro Canyon along the cascading San Ysidro Creek. The steep, narrow, upper canyon is filled with small waterfalls, continuous cascades and pools. This hike leads to San Ysidro Falls, a beautiful 60-foot waterfall.

Driving directions: From Santa Barbara, drive southbound on Highway 101 to Montecito, and exit on San Ysidro Road. Drive one mile north to Valley Road and turn right. Continue 0.8 miles to Park Lane and turn left. Drive 0.3 miles to East Mountain Drive and bear to the left. The trailhead is 0.2 miles ahead on the right. Park along East Mountain Drive.

Hiking directions: The signed trail heads to the right (north), parallel to a wooden fence. Proceed on the tree-covered lane past a few homes to a paved road. Follow the road 100 yards uphill to an unpaved road and a chain link gate. Past the gate, the trail drops into San Ysidro Canyon. At a half mile, there is a trail junction with the McMenemy Trail on the left. Continue up the canyon on the fire road past another gate and Gateway Rock, a large eroded sandstone wall on the left. A hundred yards beyond Gateway Rock, power lines cross high above the trail near another junction. Take the footpath bearing to the right, leaving the fire road. The trail gains elevation up the canyon past continuous cascades and pools. Several side paths lead to the left down to San Ysidro Creek. At 1.5 miles, a switchback and metal railing mark the beginning of the steeper ascent up canyon. The trail crosses a stream at 1.8 miles. To the right is a short side scramble up the narrow canyon to various pools, falls and cascades. Back on the main trail, continue 100 yards to a trail fork. The right fork leads to the base of San Ysidro Falls. This is our turnaround spot.

To hike further, the left fork climbs out of the canyon to the Camino Cielo Ridge, gaining 1,800 feet in 2.5 miles.

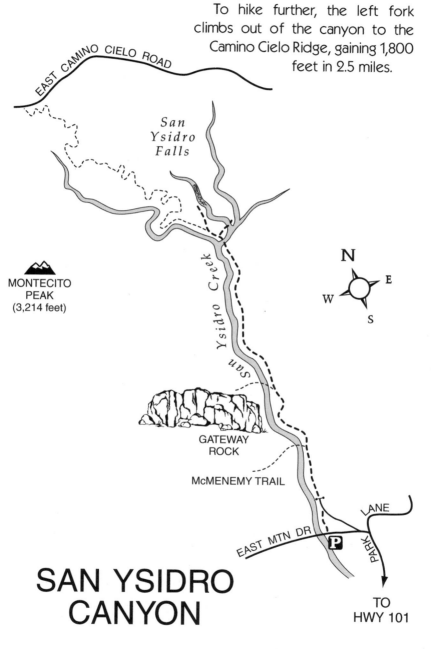

EAST CAMINO CIELO ROAD

San Ysidro Falls

San Ysidro Creek

N
E
W
S

MONTECITO PEAK
(3,214 feet)

GATEWAY ROCK

McMENEMY TRAIL

LANE

EAST MTN DR

P

PARK

SAN YSIDRO CANYON

TO HWY 101

Hike 65
San Ysidro Creekside Trail

Hiking distance: 2.4 miles round trip
Hiking time: 1.4 hours
Elevation gain: Near level
Maps: U.S.G.S. Carpinteria
        The Thomas Guide—Santa Barbara & Vicinity

Summary of hike: The San Ysidro Creekside Trail, in the heart of Montecito, meanders through an oak, olive and eucalyptus woodland. San Ysidro Creek flows through a 44-acre preserve under old stone bridges that span the creek. *

Driving directions: From Santa Barbara, drive southbound on Highway 101 to Montecito, and exit on San Ysidro Road. Drive one block north to San Leandro Lane and turn right. Continue 0.7 miles to 1710 San Leandro Lane, and park alongside the road. En route to the trailhead, San Leandro Lane jogs to the left and back again to the right.

Hiking directions: From San Leandro Lane, hike north along the east bank of San Ysidro Creek for 100 yards to an old stone bridge crossing the creek. Instead of crossing, stay on the footpath to the right along the same side of the creek. At 0.4 miles, the trail joins Ennisbrook Drive for 100 yards before dropping back down to the forest and creek. Cross the stone bridge over San Ysidro Creek, continuing upstream to a junction. The left fork leads to a cul-de-sac at the south end of East Valley Lane. Bear to the right, crossing a stream through a lush, overgrown forest. At 1.2 miles is another signed junction. The left fork also leads to East Valley Lane. Take the right fork and cross San Ysidro Creek. Once across, the trail winds through a eucalyptus forest and ends a short distance ahead at private property. To return, reverse your route.

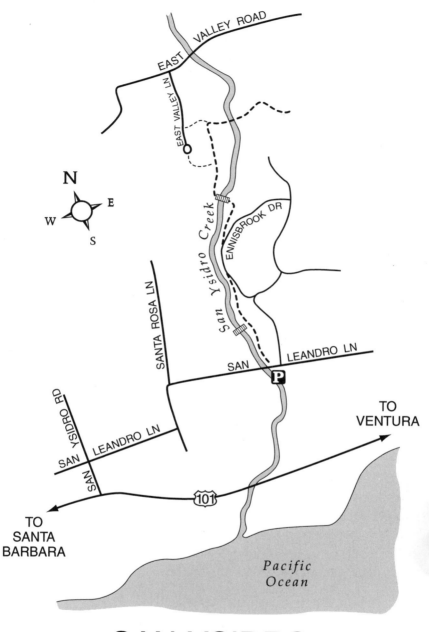

SAN YSIDRO
CREEKSIDE TRAIL

Hike 66
Summerland Beach
from Lookout Park

Hiking distance: 1 mile loop
Hiking time: 30 minutes
Elevation gain: 50 feet
Maps: U.S.G.S. Carpinteria
       The Thomas Guide—Santa Barbara & Vicinity

Summary of hike: Lookout Park is a beautiful grassy flat along the oceanfront cliffs in Summerland. From the park, paved walkways and natural forested trails lead down to a sandy beach, creating a one-mile loop. There are tidepools and coves a short distance up the coast from the beach.

Driving directions: From Santa Barbara, drive southbound on Highway 101 and take the Summerland exit. Turn right (south), crossing the railroad tracks in one block, and park in the Lookout Park parking lot.

From the south, heading northbound on Highway 101, take the Evans Avenue exit and turn left. Cross Highway 101 and the railroad tracks to Lookout Park.

Hiking directions: From the parking lot, head left (east) through the grassy flat along the cliff's edge to an open gate. A path leads through a shady eucalyptus tree forest. Cross a wooden bridge, and head to the sandy shoreline. At the shore, bear to the right, leading to the paved walkways that return up to Lookout Park. To extend the hike, continue along the coastline to the west. At low tide, the long stretch of beach leads to coves, rocky points and tidepools.

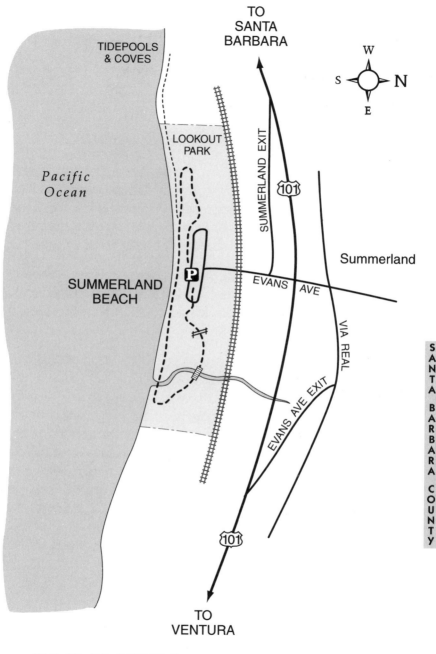

SUMMERLAND BEACH

Hike 67
Loon Point

Hiking distance: 3 miles round trip
Hiking time: 1.5 hours
Elevation gain: Near level
Maps: U.S.G.S. Carpinteria
The Thomas Guide—Santa Barbara and Vicinity

Summary of hike: Loon Point sits between Summerland and Carpinteria at the mouth of Toro Canyon Creek. Dense stands of sycamores, coastal oaks, Monterey cypress and eucalypti line the creek. The path to Loon Point follows an isolated stretch of coastline along the base of steep sandstone cliffs.

Driving directions: From Santa Barbara, drive southbound on Highway 101 to Summerland, and exit on Padero Lane south. Turn right and drive 0.2 miles to the signed Loon Point Beach parking lot on the left.

Hiking directions: Take the signed Loon Beach access trail parallel to the railroad tracks. Curve to the left, under the Padero Lane bridge, past a grove of eucalyptus trees. The path descends through a narrow drainage between the jagged, weathered cliffs to the shoreline. Bear to the right on the sandy beach along the base of the sandstone cliffs. Loon Point can be seen jutting out to sea. Follow the shoreline, reaching Loon Point in 1.5 miles. At high tide, the water level may be too high to reach the point.

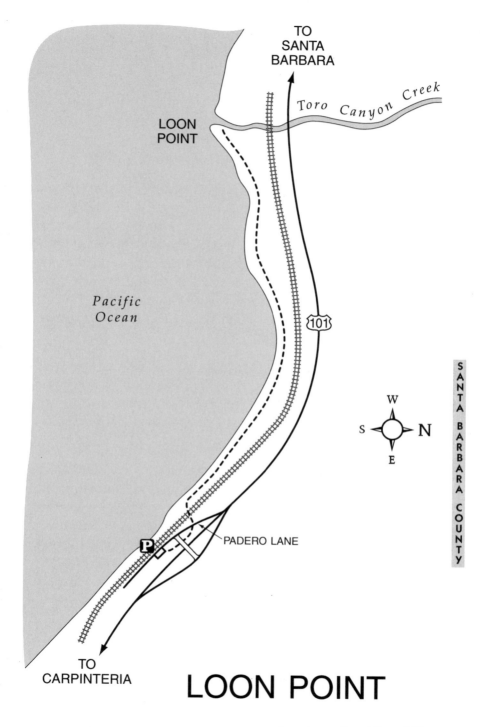

TO
SANTA
BARBARA

Toro Canyon Creek

LOON
POINT

*Pacific
Ocean*

101

PADERO LANE

P

TO
CARPINTERIA

SANTA BARBARA COUNTY

W
S — N
E

LOON POINT

Hike 68
Salt Marsh Nature Park

Hiking distance: 1 mile round trip
Hiking time: 30 minutes
Elevation gain: Level
Maps: U.S.G.S. Carpinteria
The Thomas Guide—Santa Barbara and Vicinity

Summary of hike: The Carpinteria Salt Marsh, historically known as El Estero (the estuary), is one of California's last remaining wetlands. The area was once inhabited by Chumash Indians. The 230-acre marsh is fed by Franklin Creek and Santa Monica Creek. The marsh has an abundance of sea and plant life and is a nesting ground for thousands of migratory waterfowl and shorebirds. The Salt Marsh Nature Park sits along the east end of the salt marsh with a trail system and several observation decks.

Driving directions: From Highway 101 in Carpinteria, exit on Linden Avenue. Turn right and drive 0.6 miles south to Sandyland Road, the last corner before reaching the ocean. Turn right and continue 0.2 miles to Ash Avenue. Park alongside the road by the signed park.

Hiking directions: From the nature trail sign, walk 20 yards to the west, reaching an observation deck. A boardwalk to the left leads to the ocean. Take the wide, meandering path to the right, parallel to Ash Avenue and the salt marsh. At the north end of the park, curve left to another overlook of the wetland. At the T-junction, the left fork leads a short distance to another observation deck. The right fork follows a pole fence along Franklin Creek to the trail's end. Return along the same path.

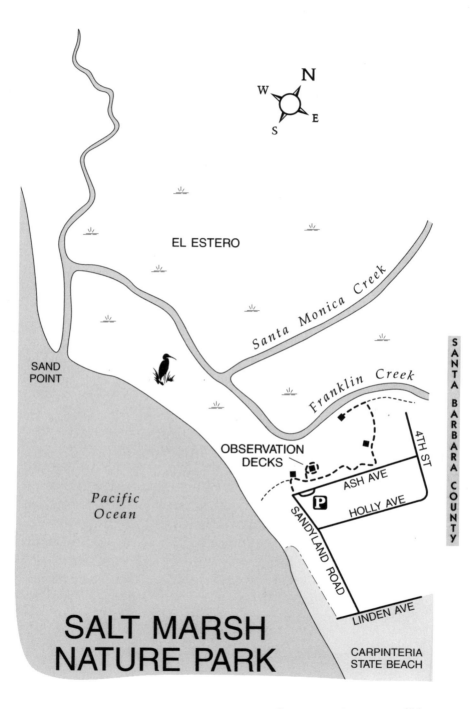

N
W • E
S

EL ESTERO

Santa Monica Creek

Franklin Creek

SAND
POINT

OBSERVATION
DECKS

*Pacific
Ocean*

P

ASH AVE

HOLLY AVE

4TH ST

SANDYLAND ROAD

LINDEN AVE

CARPINTERIA
STATE BEACH

SALT MARSH
NATURE PARK

Hike 69
Tarpits Park

Hiking distance: 1.5 miles round trip
Hiking time: 1 hour
Elevation gain: 50 feet
Maps: U.S.G.S. Carpinteria

Summary of hike: Tarpits Park is an 8-acre blufftop park at the east end of Carpinteria State Beach. The park was once the site of a Chumash Indian village. It is named for the natural tar that seeps up from beneath the soil. The Indians used the tar for caulking canoes and sealing cooking vessels. Interconnecting trails cross the bluffs overlooking the steep, jagged coastline. Benches are placed along the edge of the bluffs.

Driving directions: From Highway 101 in Carpinteria, exit on Linden Avenue. Turn right and drive 0.5 miles south to Sixth Street. Turn left and go 0.2 miles to Palm Avenue. Turn right and drive one block to the Carpinteria State Beach parking lot on the right. A parking fee is required.

Hiking directions: Two routes lead to Tarpits Park. Either follow the sandy beach east, or walk along the campground road east, crossing over Carpinteria Creek. At a half mile, the campground road ends on the grassy bluffs. From the beach, a footpath ascends the bluffs to the campground road. Several interconnecting paths cross the clifftop terrace. The meandering trails pass wooded groves of eucalypti and Monterey cypress. A stairway leads down to the shoreline. As you near the Chevron Oil Pier, the bluffs narrow. This is a good turnaround spot.

To hike further, cross the ravine, and continue past the pier along the edge of the cliffs. You will reach the Carpinteria Bluffs and Seal Sanctuary (Hike 70) in a half mile.

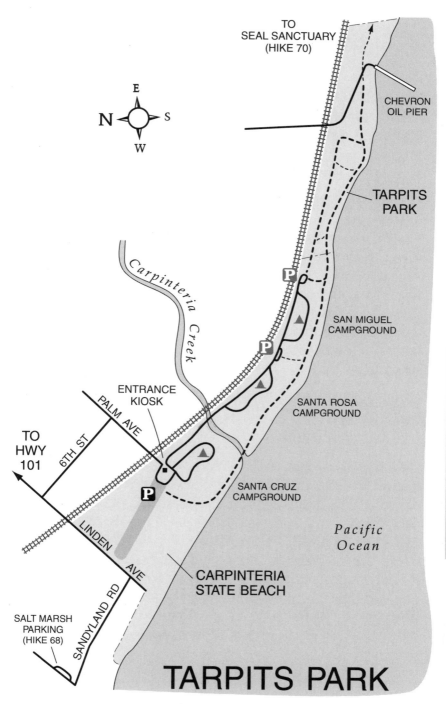

TO
SEAL SANCTUARY
(HIKE 70)

CHEVRON
OIL PIER

TARPITS
PARK

Carpinteria Creek

SAN MIGUEL
CAMPGROUND

P

P

ENTRANCE
KIOSK

PALM AVE

6TH ST

TO
HWY
101

SANTA ROSA
CAMPGROUND

P

LINDEN AVE

SANTA CRUZ
CAMPGROUND

*Pacific
Ocean*

SANDYLAND RD

CARPINTERIA
STATE BEACH

SALT MARSH
PARKING
(HIKE 68)

TARPITS PARK

Hike 70
Carpinteria Bluffs
and Seal Sanctuary

Hiking distance: 2 miles round trip
Hiking time: 1 hour
Elevation gain: Level
Maps: U.S.G.S. Carpinteria
The Thomas Guide—Santa Barbara & Vicinity

Summary of hike: The Carpinteria Bluffs and Seal Sanctuary is an incredible spot. The bluffs encompass 52 oceanside acres with grasslands and eucalyptus groves. The area has panoramic views from the Santa Ynez Mountains to the islands of Anacapa, Santa Cruz and Santa Rosa. At the cliff's edge, 100 feet above the ocean, is an overlook of the seal sanctuary. Below, a community of harbor seals play in the water, lounge and sunbathe on the rocks and shoreline. The sanctuary is a protected birthing habitat for harbor seals during the winter and spring from December 1 through May 31.

Driving directions: From Highway 101 in Carpinteria, exit on Bailard Avenue. Drive one block south towards the ocean, and park at the road's end.

Hiking directions: From the end of the road, hike south on the well-worn path across the open meadow towards the ocean. As you near the ocean cliffs, take the pathway to the right, parallel to a row of stately eucalyptus trees. At the west end of the eucalyptus grove, bear left and cross the railroad tracks. The trail resumes across the tracks, heading to the right. (For an optional side trip, take the beach access trail on the left down to the base of the cliffs.) Continue west along the edge of the ocean bluffs to a bamboo fence—the seal sanctuary overlook. After enjoying the seals and views, return along the same path.

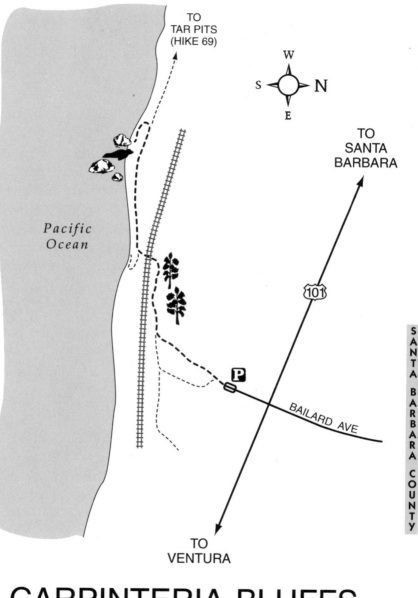

TO
TAR PITS
(HIKE 69)

W
S N
E

TO
SANTA
BARBARA

Pacific
Ocean

101

S
A
N
T
A

B
A
R
B
A
R
A

C
O
U
N
T
Y

P

BAILARD AVE

TO
VENTURA

CARPINTERIA BLUFFS
AND
SEAL SANCTUARY

Hike 71
Rincon Point and Rincon Beach Park

Hiking distance: 2 miles round trip
Hiking time: 1 hour
Elevation gain: 100 feet
Maps: U.S.G.S. White Ledge Peak
         The Thomas Guide—Santa Barbara and Vicinity

Summary of hike: Rincon Point, part of Carpinteria State Beach, is a popular surfing spot with tidepools and a small bay. The point straddles the Santa Barbara/Ventura County line. Rincon Beach Park is on the west side of the point in Santa Barbara County. The park sits on the steep, forested bluff with eucalypti and Monterey pines. There is a large picnic area, great views of the coastline and a stairway to the 1,200 feet of beach frontage.

Driving directions: From Santa Barbara, drive southbound on Highway 101 3 miles past Carpinteria, and take the Bates Road exit to the stop sign. Park in either of the lots for Rincon Point or Rincon Park.

Hiking directions: Begin from the Rincon Park parking lot on the right (west). From the edge of the cliffs, a long staircase and a paved service road both lead down the cliff face, providing access to the sandy shoreline and tidepools. Walk north along the beach, strolling past a series of tidepools along the base of the sandstone cliffs. After beachcombing, return to the parking lot. From the west end of the parking lot, a well-defined trail heads west past the metal gate. The path is a wide shelf cut on the steep cliffs high above the ocean. At 0.3 miles, the trail reaches the railroad tracks. The path parallels the railroad right-of-way west to Carpinteria. Choose your own turnaround spot.
From the Rincon Point parking lot to the east, take the wide beach access path. Descend through a shady, forested grove to the beach. Bear right on the rocky path to a small bay near the tree-lined point. This is an excellent area to explore the tide-

pools and watch the surfers. Return the way
you came.

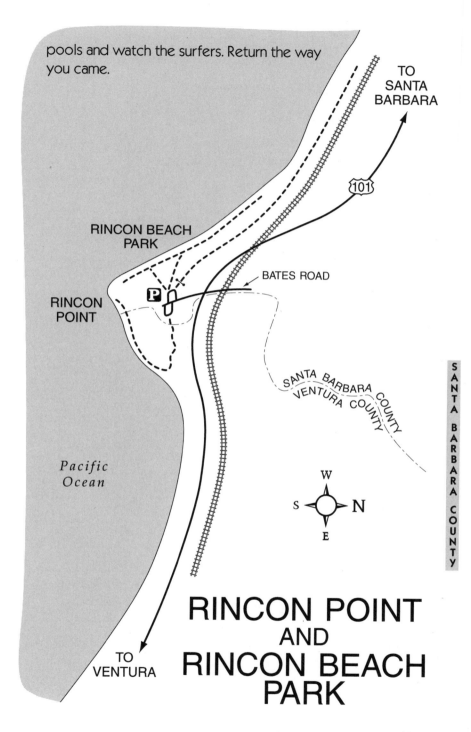

TO
SANTA
BARBARA

101

RINCON BEACH
PARK

BATES ROAD

RINCON
POINT

P

SANTA BARBARA COUNTY
VENTURA COUNTY

*Pacific
Ocean*

W

S ✦ N

E

TO
VENTURA

RINCON POINT
AND
RINCON BEACH
PARK

Other Day Hike Guidebooks

Day Hikes On the California Central Coast 14.95

Day Hikes On the California Southern Coast 14.95

Day Hikes Around Monterey and Carmel 14.95

Day Hikes Around Big Sur 14.95

Day Hikes In San Luis Obispo County, California 14.95

Day Hikes Around Santa Barbara 14.95

Day Hikes Around Ventura County 14.95

Day Hikes Around Los Angeles 14.95

Day Hikes In Yosemite National Park 11.95

Day Hikes In Sequoia and Kings Canyon National Parks 12.95

Day Hikes In Yellowstone National Park 9.95

Day Hikes In Grand Teton National Park 11.95

Day Hikes In the Beartooth Mountains
Red Lodge, Montana to Yellowstone National Park 11.95

Day Hikes Around Bozeman, Montana 11.95

Day Hikes Around Missoula, Montana 11.95

Day Hikes On Oahu 11.95

Day Hikes On Maui 11.95

Day Hikes On Kauai 11.95

Day Trips On St. Martin 9.95

Day Hikes In Sedona, Arizona 9.95

These books may be purchased at your local bookstore or
outdoor shop. Or, order them direct from the distributor:

The Globe Pequot Press
246 Goose Lane · P.O. Box 480 · Guilford, CT 06437-0480
www.globe-pequot.com

800-243-0495

Notes

About the Author

For more than a decade, veteran hiker Robert Stone has been writer, photographer, and publisher of Day Hike Books. Robert resides summers in the Rocky Mountains of Montana and winters on the California Central Coast. This year-round temperate climate enables him to hike throughout the year. When not hiking, Robert is researching, writing, and mapping the hikes before returning to the trails. He is an active member of OWAC (Outdoor Writers Association of California). Robert has hiked every trail in the Day Hike Book series. With over twenty hiking guides in the series, he has hiked over a thousand trails throughout the western United States and Hawaii.